SPARKS

OTHER BOOKS BY PETER L. BENSON

All Kids Are Our Kids: What Communities Must Do to Raise Caring and Responsible Children and Adolescents (San Francisco: Jossey-Bass, 2006)

The Handbook of Child and Adolescent Spiritual Development, with Eugene Roehlkepartain, Pamela E. King, and Linda M. Wagener (Thousand Oaks, Calif.: Sage, 2006)

Developmental Assets and Asset-Building Communities, with Richard Lerner (Norwell, Mass.: Kluwer Academic/Plenum, 2003)

Trends in Youth Development: Vision, Realities, and Challenges, with Karen Pittman (Norwell, Mass.: Kluwer Academic/Plenum, 2001)

What Kids Need to Succeed, with Judy Galbraith and Pamela Espeland (Minneapolis: Free Spirit, 1998)

Beyond Leaf-Raking: Learning to Serve, Serving to Learn, with Eugene Roehlkepartain (Nashville: Abingdon Press, 1993)

The Quicksilver Years, with Dorothy Williams and Arthur Johnson (New York: Harper & Row, 1987)

PETER L. BENSON, PHD.

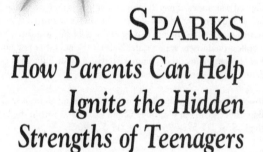

SPARKS
How Parents Can Help
Ignite the Hidden
Strengths of Teenagers

JOSSEY-BASS
A Wiley Imprint
www.josseybass.com

Jossey-Bass books and products are available through most bookstores. To contact Jossey-
Bass directly call our Customer Care Department within the U.S. at 800-956-7739, outside
the U.S. at 317-572-3986, or fax 317-572-4002.

Jossey-Bass also publishes its books in a variety of electronic formats. Some content that
appears in print may not be available in electronic books.

Library of Congress Cataloging-in-Publication Data

Benson, Peter L.
    Sparks : how parents can help ignite the hidden strengths of teenagers / Peter L.
Benson. — 1st ed.
        p. cm.
    Includes bibliographical references and index.
    ISBN 978-0-470-29404-8 (cloth)
    1. Parent and teenager. 2. Teenagers. 3. Adolescence. 4. Parenting. I. Title.
HQ799.15.B47 2008
649'.125—dc22   2008020971

Printed in the United States of America
FIRST EDITION
HB Printing   10 9 8 7 6 5 4

CONTENTS

Spark Resources

To
Liv, Kai, Brad,
Katie, Matt, Michael,
Andrew, Stef, Mike, Kyle, Maggie,
Aaron, John, Zach,
Rita, Tokie
and
TLove
The spark glistens.
Keep it at the center, always.

FOREWORD

It takes a spark to ignite the flame, that burning desire to succeed.

We as parents must ignite the spark that glows in our children as it sputters and comes to life.

As we provide our children with all the resources they need to grow into happy, healthy individuals capable of taking their place in the world, we must give them learning and growing experiences that provide that "spark," that one thing that excites and intrigues them. Then we must support that interest and help it to flourish.

Our challenge is to strike the flint that ignites the spark and then become the keepers of the flame. Feeding the fire, through our support and guidance, providing opportunities and experiences that let that flame grow until it is a glowing light—that can help illuminate the world.

Alma Powell
Chair, America's Promise Alliance

SPARKS

Introduction

How Igniting Our Teenagers' Sparks Can Support and Save Our Children and Their Future

Parenting a teenager today isn't easy. It never has been, but it's getting even harder. For the first time in many generations, parents are finding themselves dealing with overwhelming local, national, and international crises like global warming, terrorism, and financial uncertainty while at the same time wondering how they're going to raise kids who are happy and successful. The world is changing so quickly. How can we help our teenagers succeed when the future appears unpredictable—and downright scary?

I'm troubled by the many challenges our young people face today. I'm concerned about the parents who are doing their best to help their children grow up safely and achieve their true potential. That's why I've been an advocate for families and have been doing research on children, youth, and parents for more than thirty years.

I know about the difficulties—everybody does—but what I've been more interested in is what helps teenagers, their parents, and families succeed. Through my work at Minneapolis-based Search Institute, I have discovered a key way that will help all teenagers succeed, a way that makes the path clearer and brighter for each young person, for each parent, and for every family.

I call this new way of knowing and supporting our teenagers SPARKS.

> SPARKS are the hidden flames in your kids that light their proverbial fire, get them excited, tap into their true passions.
>
> SPARKS come from the gut. They motivate and inspire. They're authentic passions, talents, assets, skills, and dreams.
>
> SPARKS can be musical, athletic, intellectual, academic, relational—anything from playing the violin to enjoying work with kids or senior citizens.
>
> SPARKS get kids going on a positive path, steering them into making a difference in the world and away from self-defeating or dangerous paths.
>
> SPARKS, when they are known and acted on, help youth come to the life-changing insight that "my life has a purpose."

All our kids have SPARKS. But before we find out more about sparks and how to ignite them, let's take a closer look at the challenges our teenagers really face these days.

THE STATE OF TEENAGERS TODAY

Because the world is changing so rapidly, it's easy for parents to become confused and baffled. Our teenagers have become technological whizzes. They're talking on the cell phone while IMing (instant messaging) on the computer *and* studying for history at the same time. We ask them a question, and they don't respond because they can't hear us. Their ears are clogged with headsets or ear buds from the MP3 players hidden in their pockets. We try to connect with them, but they're out the door, with either a jam-packed schedule or a desire to be anywhere but at home.

The Plugged-in Generation

As parents, we're aware of the technological revolution, but most of our teens know far more about it than we do. They've grown up with it. They've never lived in a time when it wasn't a normal part of their daily lives. There's been nothing for them to adjust to. In fact, most teenagers think technological devices are things they *need*, not just want. Many teenagers today have a cell phone, a computer (or access to one), a video game console, an MP3 player (many of them equipped with Internet and video capabilities), and their own TV. Many use all this hardware simultaneously. When today's teenagers are awake, most of them are plugged in to something electronic.

At some point, you may have fought against these technological contraptions, raising questions about how your teenager was going to get her homework done—or even how she was going to develop *normal* social skills, such as talking to someone face-to-face or using a phone to ask questions and listen, instead of zipping off a cryptic message. You've been concerned about your teen being contacted by pedophiles and other online predators. This is awful, scary stuff, totally new and different from anything we've experienced before. We're living in a brave new world driven by technological power, and the technology itself seems to be changing every three to six months.

If we look at technology objectively, however, we can see that it's not all bad, not by a long shot. All our teenagers' technological savvy has actually had many benefits. Through the Internet and social networking sites, such as Facebook and MySpace, teenagers are connecting with teenagers around the world. They have access to television broadcasts from other countries through cable, satellite TV, and the Internet. This has led to teenagers tapping into teenage culture in other countries. Teenagers interested in Anime and Manga get most of their information from Japan and other Asian countries. Those interested in sports may root for Italy, France, or Brazil (not the United States) for the soccer world cup or for South Africa or England for the rugby world cup.

Some teenagers have embraced the food of foreign cultures and have become fond of Thai, Indian, Mexican, or Ethiopian cuisine. Some wear clothing and hairstyles that are chic with teenagers from far, far away. If you ask teenagers about their favorite music, don't be surprised if they mention a band from South Africa, Argentina, Germany, or even Saudi Arabia. They watch musical groups on YouTube, and they get ideas from people all over the world. To teenagers today, their world *is* the world.

The globalization of teenagers has led them to be comfortable with diversity, and many embrace multiplicity. A number of teenagers speak more than one language, with some of them starting a second language in preschool or kindergarten. In Southern California, more than ninety languages are spoken in the public schools. In Chicago, the number is 118. In New York City, the number is more than 120.

For some teenagers, a favorite prank is lifting a classmate's cell phone and having a bilingual (or trilingual) friend reprogram it into Mandarin Chinese, Arabic, or Russian before slipping it back to the unsuspecting teenager. The teen then cannot use the phone until he finds someone who can translate it back. Or he learns the language!

Many teens today know people of different ethnicities, races, religious traditions, political ideologies, abilities, and socioeconomic statuses. One group called themselves the "mini United Nations" because the four guys were of four different races and had four different religious beliefs: a Somali Muslim, a Caucasian Christian, a Jew, and an Asian Buddhist. This was a group of friends in a public high school—in Minnesota of all places. To these teenage boys, this group of friends was as natural as the jock or nerd group.

A Widening Gap

Yet while many teenagers are comfortable with diversity, they also recognize a growing chasm between two main groups of their peers. The rich are richer (and own fascinating technological gizmos that other teens all want). The poor are poorer. The smart are smarter (and taking college-level courses as early as seventh grade). Many struggling teenagers find themselves getting further and further behind.

There are other big chasms as well. Teenagers today know more kids who are depressed, who struggle with mental illnesses, who are trying to overcome learning disabilities, or who live in abusive or neglectful homes. Some teenagers are willing to help out, giving a poorer student the coat off their backs—only to come home to an irate parent who spouts about the high cost of clothing. They also find themselves trying to hang on to their friends (and figure out where they belong) as teenagers move away, transfer to another school, or head to an inpatient facility for a short stint to deal with mental illness or traumatic abuse.

The gap widens as many of the more affluent and privileged young people begin competing earlier and earlier. Today at middle- and upper-class preschool bus stops, many parents talk about trying to get their five-year-old kids into special language classes or elite college prep schools. With the growing competitiveness, kids are finding themselves needing to choose whether to attend an art school or a more technical school in fourth grade, seventh grade, or ninth grade, instead of waiting to make those decisions during their senior year in high school. Others find themselves on the path of being home-schooled for a number of years, attending a public school for a while, and then ending up in a private school—all before turning eighteen. Choosing what to do after high school no longer is the first big decision for teenagers today.

Instant-Results Living

For many teenagers, days are filled with smaller decisions, and many of these choices have become impulsive. Teenagers today are part of the "want-it-now generation." They don't have time to wait, and they're surrounded by devices and environments that feed their impatience and restlessness. They're used to instant messaging, and many think e-mail is too archaic, too slow, too 1990s. Many find TV boring. Why sit in front of a box when they can view downloaded TV podcasts and movies on their video MP3s—or watch clips on YouTube? All this instant access to the media makes it harder for parents to know what teenagers are watching—and when. How do you monitor a handheld device that goes with a teenager everywhere, including to bed?

Teens' expectation of quick results and instant downloading has resulted in a lot of teenagers having a sense of entitlement. Teenagers no longer believe that only certain groups should have access to certain things, based on age or authority; no, in the brave new world of open sources, everyone should have access to everything with no thought of earning it. Many expect something for nothing, and many can get a lot without doing much.

A lot of what teenagers want does have a price tag attached to it, and teenagers buy things off eBay, Amazon, iTunes, Craig's List, and Internet sites from around the world. One parent lamented how her teenage daughter's holiday wish list included items that could only be ordered online—and only from overseas.

A few groups of teenagers have special problems. For example, affluent young people sometimes wind up rudderless, believing that they don't need to do anything in life except enjoy it. Many party all the time, experiment with drugs, and often end up in despair— or in trouble.

This kind of problem is also fueled by our celebrity-driven culture. Who hasn't read the headlines about Britney Spears, Paris Hilton, and Lindsay Lohan, who spend most of their time partying and making headlines for outrageous behavior? Or about the professional athletes making headlines with their drug use, acts of violence, and arrests? Today many teenagers think that their worth is measured by how famous they can become. They brag about the number of hits their videos receive on YouTube, and they quickly learn that the more outrageous the content is, the more people want to watch.

What's even more frightening, however, is teenagers' lack of a long-term perspective. Very few people become millionaires, famous artists, acclaimed actors, or professional athletes. Yet ask teenagers if they think it's possible that they will become a millionaire, and most will say yes.

Jaded Naïveté

The events of September 11, 2001, changed not only us adults but also our children. Many teenagers today say that September 11 was a wake-up call. Only 14 percent of teenagers say, "I think the world is becoming a better place." They're worried about terrorism and the threat of global war. Among teens with a variety of political beliefs, some want to fight while others long to reach out and make peace. "About half admire America, while half don't," says Chip Walker of Energy/BBDO, which conducted research on teenagers. Some teens believe in a strong military presence and want to enlist when they're old enough. Others say the United States has been meddling too much in international affairs and causing tensions between countries to rise—instead of ease.

Although a number of teenagers stay up-to-date on current events, most are unsuspecting and naive. They're used to lock-down drills and bomb threat preparations at school, but they leave their electronic gizmos out in places where anyone can take them (and sometimes do). Although many feel unsafe in the world, they feel overly safe in certain locations, such as in teen hangouts or most teenagers' homes— or when driving cars into any kind of neighborhood.

Sexually, they're overexposed. They can easily access R- and NC-17-rated movies on the Internet—even when parents put on

Internet blockers. Pornography, hard-core pornography, is prevalent through these technological devices, which has led teenagers to dance in grinding styles, creating an uproar at school dances and with most adults. Some fashions have become much more slinky and provocative; there are more miniskirts, halter tops, and bare midriffs, leading to tighter dress codes at school, but not everywhere in the community.

For some teenage boys and girls, a hookup (a brief and casual sex encounter) can be a part of their day, like going to school. Yet while many seem jaded about sexuality, they also seem naive about date rape, sexually transmitted diseases, and the strong emotional bonds that can form from sexual intimacy. They're clueless about the depth and dimension of true intimacy as well as the conflict that can result from meaningless sex without true love or trust.

THE STATE OF PARENTS TODAY

Many grandparents shake their heads and wonder how their adult children can possibly parent well in a society that, in many ways, has run amok. Parents and grandparents have much to be concerned about. Researchers now predict that our kids will be the first generation that will not exceed the economic lifestyle of their parents, and our kids will also be the first generation in which many will not live as long as their parents, due to the high rates of obesity, diabetes, and other illnesses that result from living a sedentary, poor-diet lifestyle.

Stressors on Parents Today

All parents today—even those who are middle class or wealthy—are feeling the strain of a declining economy. Most parents are working harder, working multiple jobs, or trying to get an educational degree while also working and raising a family. Families with two parents often have both parents working different shifts (so that kids are more likely to have the presence of one parent, even though the parents rarely see each other), while single-parent families are often feeling isolated, more broke than usual, and in a state of perpetual financial anxiety.

Adding to the stress is the intensity of family schedules. Unlike the generation before us, family life doesn't necessarily revolve around one person—the old-fashioned breadwinner, usually the father—but around every family member instead. This often means juggling two careers; two jobs; kids in school with special after-class activities; huge drop-off, pickup, and commuting conflicts; and an abiding sense of tension and stress. There's just not time for everyone to do what he or she needs to do with family members running simultaneously in so many different directions.

Temptations Facing Parents Today

Because of the stress of being a parent today, many parents are finding themselves tempted to parent in ways that aren't always helpful to their kids' development. Some parents are helicopter parents, hovering closely over their teenagers to ensure that they're safe and doing the right thing. Others are demanding parents, expecting their children to be self-sufficient too early—four-year-olds caring for babies and eight-year-olds cooking (by using the microwave) to feed two or three younger siblings.

It's also tempting to slack off and let the mass media and media technology become the sole preoccupations of our teenagers, especially when that's what kids clamor to do all day. Sure, why not step back and let them post photos, make videos, watch movies, and play games 24/7? Unfortunately, too many teenagers are both spending and revealing too much of their lives online, and their parents don't even know it.

Isolation of Parents Today

Many parents feel pulled in opposite directions. They work, keep up a home, get their kids to medical appointments, and attend to school, extended family, and other activities that often lead them to wonder how they can do it all—or even do a little—in a decent manner.

This kind of stress and pressure also leaves parents feeling really isolated and alone. In a study Search Institute conducted with the YMCA of the USA, the number-one finding was that most parents felt isolated, even if they were married. Fifty-three percent of parents say they don't have any sources of support. One-third of parents said they could name only one source of support, even though research consistently shows that parents are more effective when they have lots of practical help and encouragement.

Busyness is only one barrier keeping parents from connecting with others. Another is fear for their kids' safety. A U.S. Census Bureau report found that nearly one out of every five children is kept inside because parents feel that their neighborhoods aren't safe. Yet, as the study pointed out, the crime rate has fallen, and most neighborhoods are actually safer than they were ten years ago. The problem is that we've become a fear-driven society. So much is changing, and so many bad things are happening, that it's difficult to know how to protect our children while also giving them the opportunities to grow and succeed in life.

When parents are intentional about connecting with other people, they often run into the "values tension." They discover that other parents hold different beliefs, and they're not always sure they want their children to be exposed to (or to take on) those values. Or they may run into parents who don't seem to value much of anything at all. They're disturbed that their teenagers may be highly attracted to parents who happily let them do whatever they want and to kids who have no boundaries.

Building a supportive community has become hard, and busy parents often end up focusing more on what they can control, such as their home environment, the choice of school that their child attends, and the activities that their children get involved in. Those things are important for raising healthy kids, but parents should not be doing this alone. They need community. They need support. They need others they know they can turn to—and trust.

Thus too many parents believe that if they want to get something done right, they need to do it themselves. They become superparents, attempting to do it all and driving themselves to exhaustion.

SPARKS: WHAT TEENAGERS NEED TO SUCCEED

All parents worry. It is a big and complex world to which we are introducing our children. As we try to be good parents, there are two things all of us want for our kids. We want them to know, and know deeply, that at their very core there is something good and special about them. We want them to see themselves as persons of worth, of value to the world. You and I know, as adults, what a precious gift this perception is to a person; many of us struggle with a lack of it all our lives. The second thing we want for our kids is to have the courage to put their gifts into play.

The concept of spark speaks powerfully to these universal wishes. A spark is something inside your teenager that gets him excited. It's something that makes your teenager want to jump out of bed in the morning. Spark is the thing that gives teenagers (and actually all people) meaning.

Despite all the stressors, barriers, and difficulties, a spark is something that works. Whether teenagers live in a two-parent or one-parent home, whether they're poor or rich, regardless of their race, a spark is something that works for *all* kids. A spark has the power to change the course of a teenager's life for the better.

We need to help our kids find their own sparks. We need to listen closely to what genuinely excites our teenagers. It may start with a passion for the electric guitar, tinkering with a car, shooting hoops, or another choice that we might never on our own have thought of as a way to ignite our child's inner flame. Allowing young people to follow and develop their sparks can open up other dimensions inside them that they didn't even know were there.

Why Sparks Matter

My colleagues and I at Search Institute have designed several national studies to document how sparks make a difference in the life of a teenager. What we found is this: compared to youth without sparks, youth with sparks who also have several people who know and support their sparks

- Have higher grades in school

- Have higher school attendance rates

- Are more likely to be socially competent

- Are more likely to be healthy physically

- Are more likely to volunteer to help other people

- Are more likely to be good stewards of the earth and its resources

- Are more likely to have a sense of purpose

- Are more likely to report that "I am on the road to a hopeful future"

- Are less likely to experience depression

- Are less likely to engage in acts of violence toward others

Isn't this what we want for our teenagers?

We want our teenagers to grow up well. We want them to be happy and find meaningful ways to live their lives. We want them to succeed—in all areas of their lives.

Sparks are essential.

Sparks can save our teenagers.

How Sparks Can Save Our Teens

Our extensive research into the lives of teenagers shows us that a life grounded in sparks enables a person to thrive in a changing world. Teenagers with spark feel good about themselves. They have a zest for life. Parents say that teenagers who are pursuing a spark are much easier to live with because they have a sense of purpose, a reason for being. They are on a path to a hopeful future. Even though the teen years still have their ups and downs and difficult moments, this transitional period is more meaningful and fulfilling when a teenager has a spark.

What does this mean for your teenager? And how can you, as a concerned parent, help your teenager discover and nurture her own sparks?

In Part One, I present the five basic steps for doing exactly that, helping ignite your teen's sparks:

Step One: Recognize the Power of Sparks

Step Two: Know Your Own Teenager

Step Three: Help Discover and Reveal Your Teen's Sparks

Step Four: Be the Captain of Your Teen's Spark Team

Step Five: Keep Your Teen's Spark Lit

So let us begin. Your role is crucial, as you'll see, in developing these sparks, which in turn are crucial for your teen's happiness and success.

Five Steps
to Help Ignite
Your Teen's
Sparks

STEP ONE

Recognize the Power of Sparks

spark n **1:** *an incandescent particle* **2:** *a glistening particle* **3:** *a flash of light* **4:** *a vital, animating, or activating factor*

Every teenager has a spark—something inside that is good, beautiful, and useful to the world. Sparks illuminate a young person's life and give it energy and purpose.

Sparks come in many forms. Interviews with thousands of American teenagers tell us that their sparks include writing poetry, making music, helping people, leading, being a peacemaker among friends and peers at school, making one's community better, and taking care of the earth. When our sparks glow, we feel whole. We feel useful. Life has meaning. It feels good to get up in the morning.

WHAT WE KNOW ABOUT SPARKS

Sparks are akin to the human spirit. The word *spirit* comes from the Latin *spiritas*, and is used to convey the concept of breath put into the world with vigor and courage. Spark, spirit, breath. The very essence of a person, put into play with energy and conviction.

As parents, we know when our children have a spark. You can tell by looking in their eyes. You can feel the energy, the electricity. It's wonderful to be around young people who know their sparks and put them into play.

Sparks: The Keys to Unlocking Our Purpose

So many people—teenagers and adults—live locked-up lives. They meander through life, sometimes checking things off their to-do list, but often not knowing why they are here or why they matter. When you do this too long, you get a nagging sense that something's missing, and what's missing is discovering and expressing your spark.

As noted by Stanford psychologist William Damon, one of the most prominent trends of our times is a feeling of emptiness among adolescents and young adults. Commitment and sense of direction are at risk for too many of our young. We even see it now in the burgeoning numbers of twenty-somethings living at home with their parents while they wait for something to commit to. As Damon says, we are raising teens in "a society in which purposefulness among young people is the exception rather than the rule."

Adults need to know and act on their sparks, and so do teenagers. If we can encourage young people to discover their sparks, they won't need to go through what too many of us adults go through: that wandering state of longing for something more and yearning to follow what you care about instead of doing what someone else says you should do or care about.

Sparks describes a five-step plan to help ignite your teen's spark. The plan is based on interviews with thousands of teens and parents from all walks of life: rich and poor, urban and rural, two-parent and one-parent families.

The first step is to recognize the power of sparks. Through our research, we discovered that a spark has these characteristics:

- It gives us energy and joy. We look forward to exploring it.

- When it is expressed, we feel alive. We feel useful. Life has purpose. We feel we are drawing on our best potential.

- When we are in a spark mode, we lose our sense of time. We are in the moment.

- A spark originates from inside a person. It is not imposed from the outside.

- A spark can be a skill, a talent, an interest. For some, it's a way of being in the world. And when we express it, we're not worried about how good we are or how it looks to others. Just doing it (or being it) is enough.

- Some people think of their spark as a gift, or as "the reason I am in the world."

- A spark is not just about things we like to do, like watching movies or going to the beach or working out. It is deeper than this. It is a prime source of meaning, self-directed action, and purpose in our lives.

- This is important: a spark does (or has the potential to) make the world a better place for others.

A Powerful Research Base

Through a variety of major studies of youth and families all across America, we've learned a great deal about sparks, their role in helping youth navigate through adolescence, and their impact on the health and well-being of teenagers. We've also learned about young people's *spark champions*, adults who are there for them. To create this portrait of youth, we sponsored or commissioned the following three national studies, in which we listened to the voices of more than thirty-five hundred teenagers and two thousand parents of teenagers:

- A Gallup Poll of two thousand twelve- to seventeen-year-olds and two thousand of their parents (one per teenager). This is a nationally representative sample of teenagers, with oversamples of African American and Hispanic youth.

- A twelve-question online poll of one thousand eleven- to seventeen-year-olds, conducted with the assistance of the Louis Harris polling firm.

- Interviews with 405 teenagers ages fifteen to seventeen. This was a three-day Internet-based bulletin board conversation on sparks and thriving, during which young people described their sparks, how their environments (such as family, school, and neighborhood) helped or discouraged them, what they sacrificed in order to pursue their sparks, and the ways they could tell when a teenager was thriving.

Our studies document seven major lessons about sparks, lessons that really need to become common knowledge. These lessons have the capacity to energize our families, schools, and neighborhoods to see the potential in each young person. You'll find these lessons cited throughout this book.

KEY LESSON 1
Kids Understand the Idea of Sparks and Want Them

There's no question that America's teens and young adults get the concept of spark. It is as though the idea is hardwired into their very being.

When asking about sparks, we frequently heard something like, "Oh, you mean something I am passionate about," or "Something about me that I love to do." These teens also express a desire to have sparks and can identify what having sparks looks like among their peers. The universal ease with the concept of sparks is an important discovery, one that can help generate new ways of helping teenagers grow to their fullest potential.

HOW YOUNG PEOPLE VIEW SPARKS

Young people are articulate about the characteristics of kids with sparks versus those without sparks. They have much to say, and what they say is often insightful and inspiring.

The Rich Vocabulary of Teens

When describing their own sparks, young people frequently use words like "relish," "love," "reason to smile," "passion," "sacrifice," "emotion," "commitment," "focus," "lights my fire"—the kind of vocabulary one might expect to hear from someone describing a love interest or another really important relationship. These are right-brain words of emotion more than left-brain words of reason.

There seems to be a palpable level of energy within these words. This energy has a push and a pull. The push is the named and affirmed spark. The pull is the vision of what one can be.

Examples of Teenagers with Sparks

Ask a teenager about his spark, and often he will have a lot to say. Here's how some teens from across America who have embraced their sparks describe them in an anonymous survey:

"My spark is art. I love to paint and sculpt and make things. I can take junk and make it into art."

"I love to work with disabled youth. I love seeing them be so happy at the smallest things."

"My violin is the spark that fires me up. I love music and making music. It brings so much joy to my life."

"I love helping people with their personal problems. When one of my friends is having trouble with her family, I will sit there and listen to her and help her come up with a solution."

"I am pursuing my spark by staying focused on going to school every day. Keeping my grades up. Staying away from areas that can get me pulled into trouble. I come home. I practice my music. I write lyrics all the time. I get together with the rest of my music group three to four times a week and we practice four to six hours. This is important to me because this is my spark. This is what I love. What I need to do. This will one day allow me to take care of my brothers and sisters."

"The one spark in my life that most fires me up is my love for archeology."

"I actually have more than one spark. I have loved soccer since the moment I touched the ball. It is a great way to make new friends and the thrill of playing it is so amazing to me it makes me want more. My other passion is acting. When I was younger, my dad would follow me around with a camera and I would do the funniest things. To be or to create your own perception or interpretation of a character is something I've always loved to do."

Notice that none of these statements is merely about what young people like to do. Rather, they are about what young people *need* to do. This highlights a common theme in the way young people think about sparks: a spark isn't something you go outside yourself to find. It's something deep inside you.

Teenagers with spark have an enthusiasm and passion that are almost infectious. Once teenagers get started talking about sparks, they often become philosophical and almost evangelical.

"You can try to like something because someone else wants you to, but how can you really love something if it's not something you want to do? Follow your heart and do what you love. Find your passion and go for it. It's your life and you only have one life to live." (Jamie, 14)

"If you have a spark, follow what you love and just don't give up." (Ronaldo, 13)

"A spark can be developed by finding one thing you love to do. You begin to put your all into that thing and allow it to motivate you to do bigger and better things." (Ellie, 15)

"You can find something that you love or that you are good at. Just keep trying different things until you find that spark." (Max, 17)

How a Spark Opens a New Path

A spark is about developing yourself from the inside out. It's about discovering what's deep inside you so that you're less blown around by external pressures and distractions.

Too many of our teenagers are caught up and mesmerized by what's going on outside them. They jump with every call on their cell phones. They rush home from school to see what's new on YouTube. They are dazzled by the glitter of the rich and famous. Too many are wandering aimlessly in search of things that don't connect with the deepest part of their being.

Our society promotes unrealistic expectations for young people: "You can be anything you want to be." "Anything is possible." People say these things without recognizing each individual's spark, capacity, or skills. Thus a lot of young people become discouraged because they've built their dreams on fragile foundations. They've been misled to have unrealistic or inauthentic expectations.

Not everyone can be president—or wants to be. But to pursue such a goal, you need more than desire: you also need the motivation, the deep interest, the temperament, the physical stamina, and the skills to do so. You also need others around you saying yes and helping build momentum to get you there.

The truth is, sparks often show up in places where someone finds them puzzling, or even offensive or threatening. A parent who is apolitical may find herself with a son who is emerging as an ardent Republican or Democrat. A grandparent who struggled during the Depression may have a granddaughter who volunteers at a homeless shelter and isn't interested in making money. The student who doodles and draws cartoons may baffle a parent who is a business entrepreneur.

Put a spark into action and see how it can lead a teenager to risk curiosity, wonder, and spontaneous delight. The story of Adanna does this—and more. It also provides a corrective to the too-common notion that young people are empty vessels that have to be coerced into becoming responsible, engaged, and committed human beings. Much to the contrary, we are active agents in our own development. Here's how Adanna tells it.

> When I was younger, I wasn't sure what was good and special about me.
>
> Then one day, a music teacher pointed out that there was something I really loved: singing. I sang in the choir at church and in the chorus at school, and even when I was just walking down the hallway.
>
> When I was thirteen I realized I had another spark: writing songs. I listened to all kinds of music, all kinds of songwriters, and that taught me how to write songs. For me, writing songs and playing my guitar was a way to really express myself and who I am and what I can imagine.
>
> When I was a junior in high school, a tiny cafe called the Nook caught my eye. It held open microphone

nights once a month. It was right near my school, so I'd pass it on the bus. Since this cafe was in my own neighborhood, I was curious.

So I went in to the Nook one day after school. I was sort of nervous, but something inside of me became brave, and I asked about the open mic. A guy told me to call during the day to reserve a place on the list.

When the day came, I called. There was a place for me. When I got to the Nook, I sat down. I didn't know anybody, and I began to wonder what I was doing here. The room was small, but the place was packed.

As the night went on, I found myself feeling more relaxed. The songs people sang were really good. Some were funny. Some were sad. Some were short, some were long, in all different styles.

But even with the long ones, I didn't want to leave. I was anticipating my turn. The crowd was pretty supportive.

Then they called my name.

Talk about having butterflies! But I picked up my guitar, walked away from the corner I'd been hiding in all night, and stood in front of the mic. I began to play and sing what I thought was my best song so far.

When I finished, everyone applauded. I was so happy. People came up to thank me. I felt good. I decided right then to write more and to be brave and do more performances.

A lot of people don't step out of the hidden corners of their lives. They stay in the dark because they feel they aren't good enough. Standing up in front of an audience isn't easy. Every time I do it, I get butterflies and wonder if I'm brave enough. But afterward, I know it was worth it.

This is a story of possibility and potential. It's also a story of how spark changes a life. What we see in Adanna's story is a motivation to grow and develop. And it comes from inside her, compelling her to take responsible risks, even if this means embarrassment or falling on her face. How lucky she was (and we are) that her community provided the Nook, a place hospitable to her budding talent.

Does America have enough Nooks or other settings for young people to stretch their wings? Not really. In this case, however, it was exactly this venue that enabled Adanna to step out of the shadows and let her spark shine.

KEY LESSON 2
*A Majority of Young People Have a Spark
and Can Describe It*

About two-thirds of American teenagers can name their spark and paint a picture of what it is that brings them energy, joy, and direction. Those who know it are passionate about their spark and see how their spark makes their lives richer. However, nearly twelve million young lives are waiting for the light bulb to go on.

GOOD NEWS AND BAD NEWS ABOUT THE STATE OF SPARKS TODAY

In conducting our national studies, we asked teens about their sparks in several ways. Here's one of the questions we used:

Do you have a special talent or interest that gives you joy and energy, and is an important part of who you are? When people feel that joy and energy, we sometimes say they have a "spark" in their lives. It might be writing, or science, or learning about nature, playing an instrument, being an artist, a leader, or helping others. The sparks are not just about things you like to do, like being with friends or riding a bike. The sparks give a person a sense that his or her life has a purpose or direction. Do you have sparks in your life?

What We Learned from Teenagers Who Have a Spark

How many teenagers have sparks? Among the teens we surveyed, 69 percent say they do. In the same sample, 62 percent can actually describe what their spark is; the other 7 percent can't. These numbers are both good and bad news.

SPARK FACT
The Difference by Age

The percentage of kids who say they have a spark (by age):

- 79 percent of 10- to 12-year-olds
- 65 percent of 13- to 15-year-olds
- 65 percent of 16- to 18-year-olds

The good news is that almost seven out of ten teenagers seem to have a spark in their lives. That's an incredibly important message, one that runs counter to the more common headlines about teenagers. The bad news is that 31 percent don't think they have a spark. That's a lot of kids. There are about forty million ten- to nineteen-year-olds in the United States; 31 percent translates into twelve million lives waiting for the spark in them to ignite.

How Sparks Need Help to Shine More Brightly

Here's another piece of important news. We know that teenage sparks can shine brightly or be very dim. Their brightness depends, to a large extent, on the encouragement and support the children get from the adults in their life, the *spark champions*. Yes, it's up to each individual teenager to discover and pursue her spark, but teenagers need support. They're more likely to succeed when parents and other adults encourage them and follow the ups and downs of their spark journey. Sadly, according to teens, only 37 percent of parents know and actively nourish teenagers' sparks. This is true across all demographic and socioeconomic groups.

Even though it appears that teenagers are doing well in understanding their spark, knowing doesn't always lead to action—or direction. The following stories are far too common:

> "My family is not really playing a part in helping me find my spark. And I bet that when I find it, they won't help it get going without some big-time conditions—like it has to help me be accepted into a good college or get a good job. So I'm kind of lost right now."

> "My parents are divorced, and my dad makes fun of things I do—like writing. So I don't bring it up to him."

> "My parents are so busy with their jobs. They aren't very happy. They need to find their sparks. Then maybe they could help me with mine."

> "I live in a foster home. My dad is in jail, and my mom killed herself about six months ago. In school there are some teachers who try to help, but they're too busy, so I'm usually just on my own."

To make matters worse, most teenagers tell us that there are few, if any, adults *outside* their families who affirm and nourish their sparks. No advocates, no teachers, no neighbors, no coaches, no mentors who are on their team.

We all know too many young people walking through life with too little direction and purpose. Yes, many seem busy with their MP3 players, cell phones, school activities, and video games, but busyness is not the same as pursuing a meaningful spark. Adolescence can be so much richer if sparks are kindled and nourished.

Knowing your teenager's sparks can make the time of adolescence exciting and fruitful, rather than a time to dread.

This quotation, attributed sometimes to the poet e. e. cummings, pretty well nails the power of sparks in these two sentences: "We do not believe in ourselves until someone reveals that deep inside of us there's something valuable, worth listening to, worthy of our touch, sacred to our touch. Once we believe in ourselves, we can risk curiosity, wonder, spontaneous delight, or any experience that reveals the human spirit."

So remember: this step is all about appreciating what a spark is and how valuable it can be. We parents should be searching for and listening to sparks in all our teenagers. For when our teenagers discover their spark, they discover themselves, and the world can open up to them in new ways.

Now let's go on to Step Two and learn how important it is to know our own children, so we can eventually identify and nurture all their potential sparks.

STEP TWO

Know Your Own Teenager

Because we live in a "go-go-go" society, it's easy to avoid reflection about ourselves—and our teenagers. But if we truly want to help our teenagers discover and pursue their spark, first we need to know who they truly are.

DOESN'T A PARENT ALWAYS KNOW?

It may seem strange for a parent to ask the question, "Who is this teenager I see before me?" after thirteen or more years of intimate proximity, from diapers to tattoos. Who could know your kid better than you do, you might wonder. If you don't know this teenager, who would?

But the fact is that the possible spectrum of a parent's personality, compatibility, and relationships can be quite broad. Regardless of how well bonded they feel and how much love they might have for a child, some parents just don't understand their children as well as others understand theirs.

Haven't you ever met a parent who seems like such a different type than their kid, as if they were from another planet, reaching across a wide chasm of differences in personal style or temperament? It happens! Other parents may also love their kids to pieces and feel totally tight with them, but just haven't a clue about what's going on inside that black-sweatered cocoon at this particular moment in time. Because, let's face it, teenagers are going through many changes; it's usually a volatile and dramatic transitional period, a coming of age that can create a lot of confusion all around.

That this spectrum of parental knowledge and personality exists is why it's so important to be in touch with other significant adults in your teenager's life: the teachers, grandparents, aunts, uncles, neighbors, coaches, youth organization leaders, and other adults your teenager knows. Parents who have been nurturing their teenager's spark have found that parent-teacher conferences can reveal a lot more than how their kids are doing academically. They can find out from teachers what gets their kids excited and what captures their kids' attention. Many parents have been intentional about touching base with other adults, not to snoop about their kids, but to get another adult's helpful perspective.

No matter who you ask, you will probably hear this: your child is unique. Your child has a set of interests, talents, and skills like no other teenager. Your teenager has a personality, mind, body, and soul like no other. Your teenager—even though she may not be easy to live with—is truly a gift to this world.

WHAT YOU NEED TO KNOW
ABOUT YOUR TEENAGER

Although every teenager has a spark, every teenager has a different variation of this spark. Yes, you could find a group of teenagers who name soccer as their spark, but if you were to delve deeper, you would find big variations.

One will get excited about the teamwork and synergy of soccer. Another will feel passionate about the flexibility and skill required to be the goalie. Another will get excited about controlling the ball and maneuvering through the opposition's feet to move the ball down the field. Each one participates because of the soccer spark, but each one gets fascinated by a different aspect of the sport.

Seeing What's Really There

Teenagers move in herds and sometimes act like everyone else (which, actually, is a key developmental task), yet they're also discovering aspects of themselves that are unique. Teenagers don't like to be different, and some will hide these parts of themselves in the crowd, but most won't be able to help themselves, and their true inner selves will leak out.

That's why it's important for parents to see what's really there, despite the apparent sameness of teenagers in a group. Watch what they do when they're *not* scheduled to do something. Are they reading? Talking on the phone? Surfing the Internet? Experimenting with how to make paper airplanes? Creating polls on their Facebook or MySpace page, such as rating ring tones or naming the top three worst school lunches? Banging on a drum set? Drawing cartoons on the computer?

Usually parents complain about what their teenagers are doing—and not doing. Too many teenagers spend too much time on the computer or playing video games. Most don't spend enough time doing homework, pitching in with family chores, or cleaning up their rooms. Although it's true that rules and boundaries are often a major source of conflict for parents and teenagers, how teenagers spend their free time often hints at possible sparks, and needs to be seen and studied.

Watch carefully for your child's strengths. Is your child quiet or boisterous? Both are different strengths—self-containment versus kinetic expression. Is your child artistic? Athletic? Thoughtful? A quick thinker? A problem solver? Entrepreneurial? Focused? Curious about everything? A person who saves everything? There are so many possibilities for teenage strengths.

Sometimes your teen's strengths are hard to see when you're in the mode of "picking battles." If you're in the middle of a lot of tension, analyze the tension. Sometimes your teenager's sparks are coming out in the chaos.

For example, one parent realized that his son's strength was debate because the parent was having a hard time convincing his son to make what he thought were certain positive choices—and the dad was a successful executive who rarely had problems convincing colleagues to tackle difficult tasks. Even though there was a lot of tension between the dad and his son, when the dad began to take a spark perspective, he began to see how good his son was at holding his ground, organizing his thoughts, and being persuasive. The dad relaxed somewhat about all these arguments. Yes, the two still butt heads, but the dad is waiting to see if his new perspective will turn out to be right. He wouldn't be surprised if his son studies law and becomes an attorney who's impossible to beat.

Understanding Your Child's Temperament

Your teenager's personality (or temperament) also tells you a lot about his strengths. A quiet child most likely will never become a corporate executive, but a quiet child could become an engineer who creates corporate products, or a successful painter because she enjoys spending time alone and being creative.

One of the most popular temperament frameworks around is the Myers-Briggs framework, which grew out of the work of Carl Jung. Katharine Briggs and Isabel Briggs Myers contend that there are sixteen different personality types into which all people fit. These sixteen types are identified by four major categories:

1. Extraversion versus introversion
2. Sensing versus intuition

3. Thinking versus feeling

4. Judging versus perceiving

If you look at each of these eight words, it's tempting to dismiss the framework. Everybody thinks *and* feels. Everybody judges *and* perceives. Myers and Briggs knew that. They suggest that each person has a strong disposition to operate in one way more strongly than the other. Thus a person who gets labeled "feeling" still thinks. She is simply more comfortable operating from an emotional base than from a cognitive base. The developers of this framework also believe that each one of the sixteen temperament types is equally strong. Your style just gives you more of a clue about your personality.

What's also fascinating is how your temperament and your child's temperament interact. Paul D. Tieger and Barbara Barron-Tieger wrote a book called *Nurture by Nature: Understand Your Child's Personality Type—and Become a Better Parent.* Besides helping you and your teenager identify your personality types using the Myers-Briggs framework, the authors give practical suggestions for communicating better and working together.

One mother was greatly relieved by this book. She discovered that part of the tension she experienced with her teenage son was not only that he was a teenager but also that he had a temperament that was the opposite of hers. Thus he found it relaxing to be surrounded by music and lots of friends, whereas she craved solitude. He liked to know and understand something before he made a decision, whereas she was intuitive and often made decisions based on her gut.

Appreciating Your Child's Unique Heritage

Every child comes into the world with a unique makeup. The genetic legacy of each teenager is completely different. Even twins, though there may be some remarkable similarities, are different from each other. A child's inherited physical nature, personality, and intellectual abilities all work together so that the child can become an individual like no other.

Even if you look only at your teenager's physical makeup, you'll marvel at what she has been given. Most people fit into three body types (or a combination of two or three), and the type of body you have quickly determines which paths will be easier to maneuver.

Mesomorphs are teenagers with muscular bodies. They quickly build muscle mass, and they're strong. Most athletes are mesomorphs, but so are other people who use their physical strength to pursue their spark.

Ectomorphs are the opposite. They're slim and delicate. You rarely find them on a football field. They're usually the artists, philosophers, and people who are sensitive and socially aware.

Endomorphs tend to have pear-shaped bodies that can easily become overweight. Although people with this type of body often complain about their round, curvy bodies, endomorphs tend to have excellent social skills and can organize people in ways that aren't as easy for people with other body types.

People born with disabilities sometimes question why they were born the way they were. But a number of individuals with disabilities have found unique, meaningful paths because of a spark.

Take Ken Medema. He was born blind, and as a child he felt mostly isolated and alone. Then he discovered something that really got him excited: music. Ken studied piano and voice, and he went to college to study music therapy. After working as a music therapist, he began writing and performing his own songs. He then began a successful career as a performing and recording artist. Ken believes that people can do far more than they often believe they can. Finding that unique spark helps pave the way.

SPARK TIP

Finding People Who Remember

As your child goes through changes during the teenage years, it's often easy to forget who they were as young children—and what made them unique. Look for someone who knew your child at a younger age (such as a grandparent, a coach, an aunt or uncle, or a neighbor) and ask this person what he remembers about your child. You may be surprised at what this person says. In his book *Let Your Life Speak,* Parker Palmer says we need to do more remembering of what our children were like when they were young, as those memories give important clues into who they are to become.

Thinking About Screen Time

In this time of rapid change, the world in which our teens are growing up is wildly different from the world of our adolescence.

It's easy for parents to worry about teenagers and their technology. How do you know when technology is helping them move forward—or holding them back?

Technology can clearly hurt teenagers. In some extreme cases it has been the occasion for them to move from childish pranks to outright criminal activity. We've all heard the news stories of teenagers hacking into computer systems and wreaking havoc. We've also become alarmed about teenagers secretly meeting in person the people they found online and ending up in dire circumstances. We've also heard that violent images and actions, like those in video games, can be associated with kids who perpetrate violence. The same tools that help our kids do their homework can become self-destructive, even lethal.

In response to these risks and fears, many parents try to forbid the use of the Internet or playing video games. But that's not always the best solution.

Yes, we need to keep our teenagers safe, but the technological revolution has a positive side, a side that's often overlooked. "The educational and psychosocial benefits of this type of communication can far outweigh the potential dangers," says Brendesha Tynes, a professor of educational psychology and of African American studies at the University of Illinois at Urbana-Champaign. In her research, she has found that the Internet helps teenagers

- Develop critical thinking and argumentation skills

- Find support from online peer groups

- Explore questions of identity

- Get help with homework

- Ask questions about sensitive issues they might be afraid to ask about face-to-face

- Develop skills in understanding issues from the perspective of others

Rather than seeing online interactions as a threat, Tynes suggests that parents see them as a place "allowing young people to practice interaction with others in the safety of their homes" and as a training ground for teens preparing to enter the adult social world.

Of course, this doesn't mean we allow teenagers wide and constant access to anything there is on the Internet. We can tap into the wonders of technology by continuing to talk with other adults about this issue. It's also essential to keep talking with our teenagers about what they learn on the Internet, what makes them uncomfortable, how they block others when they become wary, and how they see themselves growing during the digital age.

This doesn't mean that we set babies and toddlers in front of computers and televisions all day long. Early childhood research has clearly shown that introducing children too early to screens will hinder their development.

The American Academy of Pediatrics now recommends keeping children away from televisions and computers until age two—and even age three, if possible. When young children are old enough to be introduced to these technological devices, parents need to control the content, the time spent, and their child's frustration level. (A lot of computer games for young children are geared for a specific age and a specific skill set, for which a young child may not be ready.)

Many parents balk at not introducing the television to young children because TV can sometimes seem like a helpful distraction when parents are cooking dinner or getting siblings ready to leave in the morning. From a practical standpoint, it probably doesn't hurt to have a young child watch thirty minutes of high-quality, age-appropriate, educational programming a day, but the TV should never be a major activity for a young child.

Even as kids become teenagers, it's important to set boundaries on screen time. Too many teenagers have adopted sedentary lifestyles. When they're asked to take a break from the computer, they typically choose a different screen, such as a handheld video game or the TV.

Experts in adolescent development recommend that teenagers spend no more than two hours a day using screens. Unfortunately, for many American teenagers, two hours is a much shorter time than what they're used to spending.

SPARK QUIZ
What Do You Know About Teen Development?

How well do you understand the changes that your teenager is experiencing? How much you know about these changes affects your teenager's behavior—and your teenager's relationship with you.

Take this true-false quiz to find out how much you know. Write T if you think the statement is correct. Write F if you think the statement is incorrect.

_____ 1. Brain development is complete by the time one becomes a teenager.

_____ 2. Boys begin puberty before girls do.

_____ 3. Challenging family rules can be a normal part of the intellectual growth of teenagers.

_____ 4. The teenage years are almost always a stormy period marked by outright rebellion.

_____ 5. During adolescence, teenagers believe that friends are more important than parents.

_____ 6. When teenagers want to make more decisions in such areas as dress, curfew, and the selection of friends, they are really asking for complete independence.

_____ 7. Teenagers may experiment with potentially dangerous behaviors because they believe they cannot be harmed.

_____ 8. All teenagers sometimes do dumb things—even if they're really intelligent.

_____ 9. The types of activities kids do during the teenage years have a big impact on their development.

_____ 10. Teenagers can be mature enough to make commitments to people, ideals, or projects.

Answer key: (1) False; (2) False; (3) True; (4) False; (5) False; (6) False; (7) True; (8) True; (9) True; (10) True.

THE TEENAGE JOURNEY

When most people think of teenagers, they think "rebellion," "stress," and "turbulence." The truth is, however, that teenagers are often delightful people. They're idealistic. They're exuberant. They're creative. They have a lot of energy and drive. They see the world in a different way than adults do, and many have insightful perspectives. They are exploding into possibility—like a new star being born.

There are, of course, many pathways through adolescence. The one deeply planted in the American imagination is the one of storm and turbulence, of conflict and acting out. It's a picture that is popular in the media. The vast majority of news coverage on teenagers casts them in a bad light, covering stories of adolescent crime or rebellion far more than stories of adolescent generosity, service, and leadership.

Social science research also is preoccupied with problems, focusing more on what *prevents* drug use, teen pregnancy, violence, and antisocial behavior than on what *promotes* becoming caring, principled, engaged, and hopeful young people. The point is that in the United States, we far overstate the turbulence.

Teenagers are getting a bad rap. As Richard Lerner, one of the world's leading scholars of child development, puts it, "We do not need to see our young people as, essentially, repositories of problems." When we do, adults move away from them at exactly the time that they need adult champions. By treating teens as problems, we drive them to seek the support and acceptance of their peers while we adults go on with our busy lives.

There are three major ways that youth travel through the adolescent years.

1. For some, the theme is one of being forgotten or left behind. For far too many youth, growing up in poverty, abusive families, or a culture of crime places them in survival mode. They are vulnerable to risks and too often lack the support and opportunity needed to move forward productively.

2. Another pathway is one of boredom, of sliding by. Well-known social scientist Reed Larson has examined how youth are faring in America and comes to this conclusion: "A surprising number of youth appear to be bored, unmotivated, and unexcited about their lives. They communicate the ennui of being trapped in the present, waiting for someone to prove that life is worth living. Many youth do their schoolwork, comply with their parents, hang out with their friends,

and get through the day, but are not invested in paths into the future that excite them or feel like they originate from within."

3. A third common pathway is one in which youth are purposeful about their future and take advantage of the challenges and opportunities that life presents. They are motivated and are on the road to a hopeful future.

We could do far better in increasing the number of youth who take the third way, the journey of intention and purposefulness. To do so depends less on "fixing" teenagers and more on "fixing" the environments in which we raise our young.

As a nation, we have to do better at eliminating deep poverty and forms of discrimination that keep too many of our young people on the outside looking in. We need to re-create the places where our teens spend time so that challenge and opportunity and support far outweigh the things that cause boredom and disconnection and disengagement.

Making the third path more common starts with seeing our teens in a new and more positive way—as individuals with possibility, an inner light, a gift that our communities need. The idea is that we would do far better if we focused less on managing and controlling teenagers and more on seeing, nurturing, and unleashing their strengths.

Once we see our teenagers through this lens, we need to start showing them that this is the way to go.

Independence

In and around each of these three paths are some issues that help shape the teenage years and how you as a parent experience them. First is teenagers' march toward greater independence. That's part of their job. Teens need to learn gradually to stand on their own two feet; in so doing, they will decide what of you they will hang on to and what of you they will discard. You will always be a part of them, but they cannot be *you*. This vitally important identity work can be hard on both you and them.

Adolescent development experts have identified a number of key signs that your teenager has begun the process of achieving independence. How many fit your experience?

Choosing friends over family. Teenagers often don't like to be seen with their parents. They would rather hang out with friends or spend time with their friends' families. They think family time means they're babies doing what their parents tell them to do (which, ironically, is not how the baby stage works, despite what teenagers think).

Craving privacy. A "Keep Out" sign may appear on your teenager's bedroom door, or your teenager may close the door more often. If you ask your teenager about her day, don't be surprised if your teenager says (or gives you the look that says), "Leave me alone."

Exposing your faults. You were the superhero to your young child. Now your teenager may see you as the enemy. Teenagers have a knack for digging up your weaknesses, criticizing you for them, and even embarrassing you by pointing them out in front of other people.

Disagreeing with you. Teenagers argue about rules. They question your values. They fight about clothes, curfews, homework, meals—anything. Sometimes it may feel that the only conversation you have with your teenager is a disagreement—or an outright battle.

If you are seeing any (or all four) of these behaviors, your teenager is on the way to independence. The problem, however, is that the way adults view independence is radically different from the way teenagers look at it. Most adults equate independence with responsibility. Most teenagers say independence means freedom. These different perceptions only lead to more squabbles along the journey of living with a teenager.

Brain Development

Another fascinating feature of teenagers is what's happening to the development of their brains. We've heard a lot about the rapid explosion of brain development that occurs in the early years of a child's life (from birth to about age five), but we tend to overlook the accelerating growth that kids' brains go through during adolescence. The difference between the early childhood brain and the teenage brain, however, is that during the teenage years, the change is mainly about pruning, carving, and chiseling, rather than the expanding one sees in the early childhood years.

This pruning time doesn't mean that teenagers can't learn and grow and expand. It's more about how the brain is being sculpted into the adult brain, the way a potter molds clay on the wheel to form it into something unique and beautiful. During adolescence, the pruning involves hardwiring functional circuits and shutting down dead-end circuits.

What does all this mean to you? Here's what experts say. Expect your teenager, during this period of brain development, to be more impulsive, more emotionally volatile, and more easily unglued by stress than you might like.

Of course, hormonal changes also feed into this time of relative intensity. It's quite a mix, the combination of puberty and brain development. Scientist Ronald Dahl calls adolescence "an emotional tinderbox in which passions—both negative and positive—are ignited." As he notes, one of the most important questions parents (and teachers and policymakers) face is how the natural passion emerging in adolescence will be directed. Will it be invested in creativity and ideals and contribution, or will it be misled in the pursuit of danger and risk taking?

Teenage Building Blocks

About seventeen years ago, my colleagues and I at Search Institute devoted several years to identifying "building blocks" that help teenagers succeed in life. They are based on thousands of studies of adolescent development. I named these building blocks "Developmental Assets," and there are forty of them (see "What Kids Need to Succeed: The 40 Developmental Assets"). Since then, we have surveyed more than three million teenagers across North America and found that the more Developmental Assets young people have, the more likely they are to grow up healthy, caring, competent, and successful.

What else have we found with this rich research base? The more Developmental Assets teens have,

- The less likely they'll get into trouble (using drugs, having sex, skipping school, and so on)

- The more likely they'll act in ways we value (for example, helping others, succeeding in school, and exhibiting leadership skills)

- The more likely they'll bounce back from difficulties (recovering from a long illness or accident, or coping with a loss or tragedy)

Teens and Adult Relationships

Now here is something that might seem ironic. Teens covet strong and positive relationships with parents and other adults precisely at the time they may give off signals that contradict this. It's just that the rules of engagement are changing. Teens want less to be bossed around by adults and more to engage in real conversation that starts from the idea that "I'm okay, you're okay" rather than "I'm okay, you're not okay."

The 40 Developmental Assets cover a big territory, including support, empowerment, boundaries, positive values, and social competencies. Where do these building blocks, these assets, come from? More than anything, they have been encouraged by adult relationships in which parents, teachers, neighbors, coaches, and others treasure a young person, seeing him as worthy of respect and having capacities that are good, beautiful, and useful to the world.

Relationships are the oxygen of human development. But here's the rub: according to my studies of several million teenagers, most teenagers lack these kinds of relationships with adults. What this means is that a teenager's spark is too often unseen and undernourished.

Let's put this in perspective. Sparks emerge in a teenager's life at exactly the right moment. They emerge while teenagers are forming their identity. They emerge while teenagers are struggling with independence and seeking to find a purpose in their life. It's as though nature has given teenagers a bridge to the future and a golden opportunity for parents and other adults to see them in a new light. It's exactly the right moment for parents to go inside young people and help them capture, explore, and express their inner light.

Both boys and girls are waiting for these relationships with you and all the other significant adults in their lives. We can choose to manage and control teens—or we can choose to let them find their light, their spark.

SPARK FACT
The Difference by Gender

The percentage of kids who say they have a spark (by gender):

- 73 percent of girls
- 64 percent of boys

Knowing your teenager is only one step, but it's a critical step that helps you lead her in the right direction, in the direction of living a life illuminated by sparks.

STEP THREE

Help Discover and Reveal Your Teen's Sparks

Walk into any large bookstore and check out the self-help section. You'll see an abundance of books for fifty- and sixty-year-olds about finding one's passion in the second half of life. The message in these books is that it's time, at fifty or so, to get off the treadmill of pursuing status, position, security, prestige, or money and reorganize your life around the things that bring you joy and quality of life for the last third or so of your existence.

This message is, of course, very akin to the concept of sparks. It's good for senior adults to slow down, reassess, and get on a new path that can give them more fulfillment and success in the final years of their life. But it's also tragic—individually and nationally—that we fail to think about (or promote) a thriving lifestyle between the birthing room and midlife or retirement, that we don't focus this kind of energy on that stage of life that appears to be so difficult and often filled with unhappiness: the teen years.

LAUNCHING TEENS' SPARKS

One of my personal goals is to mobilize parents to help teenagers experience adolescence and enter adulthood on a thriving path rather than making them wait thirty or forty years until they too scour a bookstore looking for insight about making a course correction in their lives.

Unfortunately, we've created a couple of patterns in our conventional society that are far from healthy. One pattern is that we take the path of not knowing our passion—what we really want to do—and consequently wander for a long time, moving from job to job or from household to household, getting out of the messes we find ourselves in and hoping for something better. Or we know our secret spark, our greatest love, but think "Oh no, doing that wouldn't be responsible," so we focus instead on generating an income, creating a home, and starting a family—all at the expense of snuffing out our spark.

Starting on the Spark Path

It's time to carve a new path, the spark path. This doesn't mean that we should encourage our teens to shirk their more conventional responsibilities; far from it. It does mean, however, that we help our children weave a life tapestry that includes their sparks and their hopes, as well as their responsibilities.

So what are your child's sparks? For some parents, that's an easy question. But for many of us, it's going to take a bit of digging. Much of the difference, of course, has to do with the teens themselves. Every kid, as we saw in Step Two, is different and unique. Some know exactly what their sparks are and pursue them with a passion. Others have a sense of what their spark *could* be and are experimenting. Still others may think they don't have any sparks at all. Even among the kids who do have sparks, some wear them on their sleeves, and others keep them hidden. Don't worry. We'll figure it out together.

What Were Your Sparks?

The old adage that "it takes one to know one" applies nicely when it comes to sparks. Parents who know and embrace their own spark are much more likely to understand and nourish sparks in their children. So to begin uncovering, nurturing, and igniting your child's sparks, think back to your own teenage years (roughly between the ages of twelve and eighteen).

You have the luxury of perspective here. You are likely to be able to see things about your teenage years now that you couldn't see then. All of us, I'm sure, have things about those years we'd like to forget. But there are also things about those years that are worth naming and celebrating—people who mattered to us, moments of grace and generosity, turning points, *and* the signs and symbols that there was something about us that was hopeful and good and useful to the world.

SPARK SELF-TEST
Your Sparks

The following questions for adults are from our national poll. Take a few moments now to answer them yourself. Consider also asking for input from another significant adult, such as your mom, dad, sister, brother, or close friend, who knew you when you were a teen.

1. Did you have a spark or sparks at age sixteen?
   ☐ Yes
   ☐ Not sure
   ☐ No
2. What was (were) your spark(s) at age sixteen?

   _____

   _____

   _____

3. Which of these people gave your spark *a lot* of support, affirmation, and encouragement? (Check each that applies.)

   ☐ My mother
   ☐ My father
   ☐ A teacher
   ☐ A friend my age
   ☐ A grandparent
   ☐ A youth worker or youth leader
   ☐ An aunt or uncle
   ☐ A neighbor

Keep your answers in mind as you read on!

Key Results from Our Survey of Adults

In our national poll of adult thriving of 1,112 parents of ten- to eighteen-year-olds, seven out of ten participants (71 percent) said they had one or more sparks at age sixteen; 18 percent said they were not sure, and 10 percent said they had no spark at sixteen. Interestingly, our ability to recall and name our sparks seems to get clearer as we mature. Whereas 71 percent now say they had a spark at age sixteen, only about half of them report that they recognized it in themselves at the time.

What else did we learn about sparks from our study?

- Of those adults who know their sparks, 57 percent act on them every day or nearly every day, and 37 percent express the spark "sometimes or once in a while"; 6 percent say they "never or rarely" put their sparks into play.

- 95 percent say having sparks in their life is very or extremely important.

- 61 percent say they have many friends who "see and appreciate my sparks."

- 81 percent wish they could express their sparks more than they currently do.

The way people name their teenage sparks is, frankly, all over the place—as it should be. Together the sparks weave a beautiful tapestry of strength and capacity and energy. The following is a sample of sparks that come from our national poll of adults.

- Painting
- Drawing
- Sculpting
- Making things with my hands
- Repairing things
- Singing, choir
- Playing an instrument
- Being in a band or orchestra
- Playing a sport I love
- Creative writing
- Public speaking
- Being in nature
- Preserving the natural world
- Photography
- Dance
- Drama, acting
- Learning languages
- Learning about history
- Learning about other cultures
- Math
- Science
- Reading
- Working with or caring for animals
- Growing things
- Leading
- Politics
- Creating new ideas
- Inventing
- Organizing things or people
- Helping people
- Making my community better
- Volunteering
- Helping children
- Growing my spiritual life
- Counseling

- Tutoring
- Studying people
- Coaching
- Sewing, knitting, crocheting
- Sailing
- Cooking

- Designing clothes
- Writing music
- Writing rap or other song lyrics
- Teaching someone a skill (such as swimming)

IDENTIFYING YOUR TEEN'S SPARKS

Now that you've got a handle on your own sparks, you're ready to taking a look at your child's. In so doing, keep in mind some of the criteria we discussed earlier. A spark is a source of energy and joy. It's a good thing, a useful thing, although whether or not it will have long-term utility at this point in your kid's life isn't necessarily important. It's a skill, interest, or capacity worthy of being nurtured. It motivates your child in a positive way.

Assessing Your Teen's Sparks

Following are three more questions for you to answer. If you have a spouse, partner, or another significant adult in your life who knows your child well, it would be useful for him to answer them too. But do so separately. After you've finished, come back together and share your answers. You may think you have a pretty good idea of what gets your child excited and what shuts him down. But I'm betting you'll be surprised at the differences between the two sets of answers.

-----

1. What are your child's current or potential sparks?

_____

_____

_____

2. When did you first understand about or see these sparks? Are they new, or did they show up earlier? When?

_____

_____

_____

3. Who are the adults who know and support your teenager's spark? What do they do to help the spark shine?

a. _____

b. _____

c. _____

d. _____

At this point, you've relived a little of your past and rekindled the sparks of your youth (or at least the memories of them), and you've taken your best guess at what your child's sparks are.

That's all fine as far as it goes, but you're really just speculating. Next you'll need to talk to your teen about what she thinks about sparks, if she does at all.

As the parent of a teenager, you know that getting your child to sit down with you for a serious discussion may not be easy. For that reason we suggest that you ask your teen to take the following survey—which we've given to hundreds of teens across the country—on his own. It's only eleven questions long and shouldn't take more than ten minutes to complete. But the results are often very revealing and can lead to some powerful changes. So just make a copy of these pages or hand this book over to your teen and ask him to find you after completing and scoring the survey.

The Spark Self-Assessment

1. Do you have a special talent or interest that gives you joy and energy and is an important part of who you are?

   ☐ a. Definitely
   ☐ b. I think so
   ☐ c. Maybe
   ☐ d. No

2. Which of the following best describes you?

   ☐ a. I feel happy and energized all the time.
   ☐ b. I feel happy and energized when I do one or two special things.
   ☐ c. I sometimes feel happy and energized.
   ☐ d. I hardly ever feel happy and energized.

3. When people have a special talent or interest, we sometimes say they have a "spark" in their life. A spark is something they're passionate about; it really fires them up, gives them joy and energy, and is an important part of who they are. It doesn't really matter what the spark is, just as long as it gives life purpose, direction, meaning, or focus. How often do you have this kind of spark in your life?

   ☐ a. Every day
   ☐ b. Most days
   ☐ c. Sometimes
   ☐ d. Hardly ever

4. How many sparks do you think you have? A spark can be doing art, learning another language, volunteering, playing a sport or a musical instrument, taking care of animals, reading, using a computer to do creative things, fixing or building something, and so on.

   ☐ a. Three or more
   ☐ b. Two
   ☐ c. One
   ☐ d. Zero

5. What are your sparks? List each one.

_____

_____

_____

_____

6. How often do you develop, use, or express your interests, talents, or sparks?

☐ a. Every day
☐ b. Most days
☐ c. Sometimes
☐ d. Hardly ever

7. Which statement is most true about you?

☐ a. Ever since I was young, I've always had some kind of spark in my life.
☐ b. I first discovered my sparks a few years ago.
☐ c. I'm just now learning what my sparks are.
☐ d. I've had sparks before, but I don't right now.
☐ e. I've never really had any sparks in my life.

8. How much do you agree or disagree with this statement? *I set goals about developing and getting better at my sparks.*

☐ a. Strongly agree
☐ b. Agree
☐ c. Disagree
☐ d. Strongly disagree

9. How much do you agree or disagree with this statement? *I am not afraid to talk about my sparks or show people what my sparks are.*

☐ a. Strongly agree
☐ b. Agree
☐ c. Disagree
☐ d. Strongly disagree

10. How much does this statement describe you? *I feel a sense of purpose or meaning in life.*

    ☐ a. This is a lot like me.
    ☐ b. This is sort of like me.
    ☐ c. This is a little like me.
    ☐ d. This is not at all like me.

11. How much does this statement describe you? *I believe I am going to make a difference in the world.*

    ☐ a. This is a lot like me.
    ☐ b. This is sort of like me.
    ☐ c. This is a little like me.
    ☐ d. This is not at all like me.

Scoring and Assessing the Results

Go back to question 5. If you named four items, count it as an A. If you named three, it's a B. If you named two, it's a C. If you named one, it's a D. If you didn't write any, it's considered an E.

For each of the questions, give yourself 4 points for each A. Give yourself 3 points for each B. Give yourself 2 points for each C. Give yourself 1 point for each D or E.

Then add up your total score.

37–44 points: Excellent. You know your spark, and you're pursuing it. Continue to move forward. Learn more about your spark. Find support. Go even deeper. Focus on mastering your skills to make your spark shine even more.

29–36 points: Good going. You know your spark, but you could spend more time pursuing it. What's holding you back? Identify any barriers and try to work around them.

21–28 points: You're just getting started. You may have a sense of what you're interested in, but right now you're just dipping a toe into the water. What do you need to do to dive in and find out more about your spark? Who can help you along the way?

Less than 21: What are you overlooking? Maybe you've never thought you had a spark. Maybe you had a spark at one time but don't have one anymore. Having a spark will add more joy and excitement to your life. Whom could you talk to about finding your spark? Which activities could you try that might interest you?

———————

If your teenager scored 29 points or more on the Self-Assessment Spark Scale, congratulations. She already has a sense of what gets her excited, and that's good news. Your role now is to support and encourage your teenager to go deeper with her spark, and to keep tabs on her journey. Following a spark is not like climbing a ladder. It's more like climbing a mountain, and most climbers will tell you that the way to the top is rarely straight up, but rather a serpentine path that weaves its way up, down, and around.

If your teenager scored 28 point or less, don't be discouraged. Many teenagers go through phases when they aren't sure what their sparks are, just as adults do. This is a time when kids are struggling to fit in but also trying to stake out their territory as individuals. They're also spending a lot of time reflecting and trying to reinvent themselves. Throw in puberty and you've got a situation that can be confusing and trying for everyone—including you.

Talking the Talk

A key way to help your teenager discover his spark is to talk about spark. The questions that follow are excellent conversation starters. But before you start asking, give them a quick read-through and think about how *you* would answer them, in case your teen turns the tables to ask you the same questions—and there's a very good chance he will.

- What makes you want to jump up out of bed in the morning?

- What makes you dread getting out of bed? (Sometimes talking about the things that aren't your spark can give you clues about finding it.)

- Which day is your favorite day of the week? What do you look forward to doing that day?

- If you could spend a whole day doing anything you wanted, and money and resources were unlimited, what would you do? Why?

- What makes you feel really happy?

- What is your special talent?

- What are you interested in doing (or learning)?

- What have you done that you're most proud of? Why?

- Who are your adult role models? Why?

- What do you think is your purpose in life?

SPARK TIP
A Moving Conversation

Because sitting down and talking about sparks may not be easy at first, it's a good idea to find the right moment, a time that's not formal and self-conscious but rather spontaneous and relaxed.

A great time to initiate a conversation about spark is when you and your teen are in the car, subway, or bus, moving forward shoulder to shoulder. There's something about being physically close together but not actually looking at each other that often makes it easier for teens to open up—their mouths as well as their ears. Try going for a ride or a walk together. Work on a project side by side. Do whatever you can to break the ice and talk about the sparks in their lives.

Most Common Categories of Sparks

Here's one more little quiz (I promise, this is the last one in this chapter). Which of these spark categories do you think is the most common among teenagers?

- Athletics

- The creative arts (painting, writing, dance, music, acting)

- Nature, ecology, the environment

- Learning a subject, such as science or history

- Helping, serving, volunteering

- Leading

- Spirituality or religion

- Animal welfare

- Being committed to living in a specific way (with joy, passion, caring, or the like)

- Reading

The hands-down winner is creative arts, by a margin of almost two to one over sports (which ranks second). Let's think about this for a moment. The creative arts lend themselves to personal expression; they are usually not competitive the way athletic activities are. One can feel competent in this domain without the stress of striving to meet certain external pressures such as how fast, how far, how many wins, and how many points. The motivation for creative expression is almost always intrinsic (that is, the act is its own reward).

Certainly, sports participants can also experience this same kind of intrinsic motivation. People of all ages love to feel the excitement of movement, the joy of physical activity, the rush of pushing themselves to do more and better with their bodies. But it is just as likely that the engagement is driven by external factors—competition, peer pressure, parental pressure, and the quest for public attention and popularity, for example—which lack the "joy factor" that creative expression can so easily generate. The creative arts also have the advantage of allowing a freedom of expression through which young people gain power or control over their world.

Now here's the problem. Our communities and schools invest far more in sports programs than in music, art, drama, and other creative arts. As a matter of fact, when money gets tight (which happens all too often), arts programs are the first to get the axe, long before sports. In my view, it shouldn't be an either-or situation. As a nation, we should be investing as much as we can in any kind of activity that enables youth to express their spark.

Table 3.1 lists the percentages of young people who claim sparks in the ten major spark categories named by youth in our national studies. The percentages for all youth add up to more than 100 percent because teens, on average, report 1.4 sparks.

The Value of Sparks

The information in Table 3.1 paints an impressive and compelling picture of how teenagers engage with life. Remember that sparks represent an aspect of the self that is deeper than just interests or hobbies and favorite ways of having fun or passing the time. The criterion for naming something a spark is a kind of natural power for unleashing energy, joy, and passion. That means sparks are getting at something a little deeper . . . something like an anchor.

There are two other things we should value about the list of sparks. First, each of these ten spark areas has the potential to connect youth with caring and principled adults who share the same passion. That connection both deepens the sparks *and* generates collateral benefits, such as support and affirmation and challenge, each of which we all need to grow and develop.

Second, each of these sparks, when alive and put into play, can have great benefits for our communities and our society. We need young people to make music, to express our humanity through art, to be generous to others, to be stewards of the earth and its creatures, to be grounded in spirit, and to lead.

This profile of sparks tells America an important story. Many teens are *not* self-absorbed, irresponsible social problems. No. With new eyes, we see that teenagers are, by and large, the gifts we need to make our world richer.

Table 3.1: Ten Major Categories of Sparks

	All Youth (%)	Boys (%)	Girls (%)	Ages 12–14 (%)	Ages 15–17 (%)
1. Creative arts (music, art, drama, dance, and so on)	54	43	65	54	55
2. Athletics	25	37	16	29	21
3. Learning (academic subject areas)	18	18	18	18	17
4. Reading	11	9	13	10	12
5. Helping, serving, volunteering	10	7	13	10	11
6. Religion, spirituality	10	8	12	9	11
7. Nature, ecology, environment	8	10	6	10	5
8. Being committed to living in a specific way (with joy, passion, tolerance, caring, or the like)	7	7	7	7	7
9. Animal welfare (caring for, advocating for, protecting endangered species, and so on)	6	2	8	7	4
10. Leading	2	2	2	2	3

KEY LESSON 3

Expand Your View of What Sparks Can Be

It's tempting to think that all sparks are in the arts, sports, and in other well-known extracurricular activities. Although many sparks fit these categories, there are a number of teenagers who find unusual sparks that are just as important, such as entrepreneurial sparks, mechanical sparks, people-organizing sparks, and technical sparks.

FOLLOWING YOUR BLISS

Joseph Campbell, the great interpreter of world mythology, knew about the power of sparks when he said, "Follow your bliss." A spark is something deep inside you that brings you joy, that gets you excited, that unleashes your spirit. When people ask, "What is my teenager's spark?" I say it's something that's uniquely theirs, and when they find it, they'll know it. And you'll know it, too.

Three Different Flavors of Sparks

Teen sparks generally come in three flavors:

- Something they're good at—a talent or skill—like piano or soccer or writing.

- Something they care deeply about—such as the environment, animals, helping people, or serving their community.

- A quality that they know is special—such as caring, listening, empathy, or being a friend.

As you go through the process of helping your teenager discover her spark, expand your view of what a spark could be. Sometimes an authentic spark may be something you don't recognize or have never even heard of.

That's what happened to Julia, whose teenage daughter insisted that Julia buy her an ocarina. At first, Julia had no idea what an ocarina was. As Julia and her daughter, Linnea, looked into the subject, Julia learned that an ocarina was an ancient flute-like instrument. When Julia asked where Linnea had learned about it, Linnea said that the video game *Zelda* had a main character, Link, who played the ocarina. Linnea thought it was the most beautiful-sounding instrument she had ever heard and became obsessed with the idea of learning to play it.

The local music stores didn't have an ocarina, but Julia finally found the instrument through an online music store. She ordered it, and Linnea started playing the minute the package arrived. Because there were no music teachers who taught the instrument, Linnea searched the Internet and found instructions on how to play it.

SPARK FACT
First Glimmers

At what age does a child's spark typically appear? Here is what was reported in an online Search Institute survey of more than eleven hundred parents:

Age When Spark Appeared	%
Birth to 3	11
3 to 5	17
6 to 9	25
10 to 12	21
13 to 15	18
16 to 18	8

Sparks can even develop out of activities that others find distasteful. Take the case of Leah Adler, who was a little concerned about the behavior of her son, Steven. He cut off the head of one of his sister's dolls and gave it to her on a bed of lettuce. Once, when his parents asked Steven to paint one bathroom wall, he painted *everything in the bathroom*—including the toilet and the mirror. Their struggle with Steven went on and on.

Then Steven joined the Boy Scouts. For some reason, Steven became fixated on the merit badge for moviemaking, so his father bought him a Super-8 camera. When Steven made a full-length movie and convinced a nearby theater to show it, his mother put up the letters on the marquee and was relieved that Steven had finally found a hobby.

Then Steven said he needed his mother's kitchen to shoot a scene for another movie. His mother agreed, bought thirty cans of cherries, and helped Steven cook them in a pressure cooker. Leah was thrilled that Steven was filming a movie about cooking, but Steven wasn't interested in just cooking these cherries. He wanted to film *exploding* cherries. Leah said that for years after that, she had to wipe off the cherry residue every time it oozed up from the wood in her cabinets.

Today Leah is relieved that Steven is grown, but she also knows that a lot of this perplexing behavior has made her son who he is today. Most people now know about Leah's son, the famous film-maker Steven Spielberg, even if they've never actually met him.

A World of Sparks

Expand your view of sparks by looking at even more categories. Considering how rapidly our world is changing, we expect new sparks to be developed constantly. In "Teenage Sparks: A Rich National Tapestry" in the Spark Resources section of this book, we list about two hundred sparks that have been named by youth from all over the United States.

Here's a sample:

- Art (painting, pottery, drawing, illustrating, sculpture, and more)

- Athletics (archery, badminton, baseball, basketball, broomball, cross-country skiing, dance, diving, down-hill skiing, floor hockey, football, golf, gymnastics, hockey, individual conditioning, lacrosse, racquetball, soccer, softball, swimming, table tennis, tennis, Ultimate Frisbee, volleyball, water polo, weight lifting, and more)

- Building (drafting, woodworking, cabinetry, construction, and more)

- Computers (keyboarding, computer programming, computer software, computer hardware, computer peripherals, computer repair, and more)

- Drama and theater (acting, directing, lighting, set design, and more)

- Entrepreneurship (creating businesses, developing new products, designing services, and more)

- Languages (American Sign Language, Arabic, French, German, Hebrew, Mandarin Chinese, Spanish, and more)

- Leadership (student government, civic decision making, motivating people, conflict resolution, and more)

- Learning (math, language arts, science, political science, history, geography, and more)

- Mechanics and engineering (electronics, bridge and highway design, auto mechanics, car audio, machine repair, customizing, and more)

- Music (choir, band, orchestra, jazz band, wind ensemble, rock bands, and more)

- Photography and film (nature photography, videography, animation, digital photography, filmmaking, and more)

- Relationships (making friends, supporting friends, being a peacemaker, empathizing, social networking through technology, and more)

- Solving social problems (global warming, poverty, racism, at-risk children, pollution, and more)

- Writing (poetry, short stories, fiction, nonfiction, essays, journal writing, and more)

Remember that sparks emerge in dozens of different ways. What's common is that the spark always has an internal resonance. That is, once it's identified, a spark feels as if it comes from the inside. But it often has to be awakened. There are lots of ways this happens. The trick, however, is that the process isn't always smooth.

Keep in mind that in the discovery process, some young people will

- Be attracted to so many different things that it seems they have a "spark a day" or a "spark a week"

- Seem not to be drawn to anything

- Go through periods when they focus on a spark and then have periods when they seem to lose interest in the spark

So don't fret if the initial dialogue hits a wall. You've made important progress just by introducing the idea of sparks and providing examples and encouragement for your teen to enter the discovery process.

SPARK FACT
The Three Most Common Sparks

Boys
    Creative arts: 43 percent
    Athletics: 37 percent
    Learning (history, science, literature, and so on): 18 percent

Girls
    Creative arts: 65 percent
    Learning (history, science, literature, and so on): 18 percent
    Athletics: 16 percent

How and Where Sparks Can Be Ignited

A spark can be lit from just about anywhere. The book *Passionaries: Turning Compassion to Action* highlights a number of teenagers whose sparks were kindled in some unusual ways:

- *A magazine article.* Eleven-year-old David Levitt needed to find a community service project to do as part of his bar mitzvah. He happened to read an article in *Parade* magazine written by the founder of the Kentucky Harvest project, which focuses on "foodraising" instead of fundraising. That magazine article started David on his quest to collect leftover food from school cafeterias and food suppliers and provide it to homeless shelters and free food kitchens for the poor. Instead of completing just the one community service project that he was required to do, that one project led to much more. David is passionate about feeding the poor—and he continues to do so today.
- *A challenge by a parent.* Fifteen-year-old Shauna Fleming was challenged by her dad to get her school to do something positive for those serving in the military. Shauna started a national campaign to generate one million letters and e-mails to current and former military members. She called her campaign "A Million Thanks."
- *Eavesdropping.* Eight-year-old Brandon Keefe was sick, and his mother needed to bring him along to a meeting that she couldn't cancel. As Brandon sniffled and played a handheld video game, he heard someone mention that the children's home needed books for its library. The next day at school, the teacher asked the class to brainstorm community service ideas. Brandon's hand shot up, and he told them about the children's home's needs. When the fund drive was done, the school had collected 847 books to donate.
- *A school assignment.* Wendy Kopp needed to write a persuasive paper, and she was stumped. What could she write about? What needed changing? As she began her research, she stumbled upon a topic that captured her attention: too many kids weren't getting high-quality education through their schools. So she decided to found Teach For America (TFA), where bright, civic-minded col-

lege graduates would teach in a challenged public school. Today, TFA draws thousands of applicants each year.

- *Television.* Eleven-year-old Trevor Ferrell was shocked when he saw a TV news story about people who lived and slept outside. He convinced his parents to take him to a homeless person sleeping on the street in his community, to whom Trevor gave away his blanket and pillow. After that, Trevor's passion grew, and his family helped him prepare hot meals and sandwiches for a hundred people every night. Now, twenty years later, the work Trevor started continues through Trevor's Place, a transitional housing nonprofit that has nineteen affiliate chapters across the country.

- A *natural disaster.* Fourteen-year-old Michael Spencer volunteered to help when a tornado struck his hometown in Arkansas. After helping provide shelter, food, and medical help, he was hooked. He became a CPR and first-aid instructor and a lifeguard trainer. He organized blood drives and raised money for charity during the holidays. When he went to college, he spent all his school breaks and summers volunteering full-time for the national Red Cross headquarters.

Sometimes a news story can ignite a spark in a young person. "When I was twelve, I heard that slavery was still going on in many parts of the world," says Zach Hunter. "And I felt that I couldn't sit by and let this sort of thing happen. I felt that it wasn't enough to feel bad." Zach began asking students at his school to contribute loose change to nonprofit antislavery organizations. Zach also looks for every opportunity he can to speak out on the matter, because it's something he believes needs to change.

SPARK TIP
Finding Inspiration for Sparks from Elders

A really useful way to help kids identify sparks is to have them interview an "elder" in their life. That could be a grandparent, a great aunt or uncle, or some other older person in your extended family (or in your neighborhood, church, synagogue, or mosque). Encourage your teenager to copy the following questions and ask this person about her or his sparks.

- When you were a child, what was your spark?
- When you were an adult, what got you excited? Why?
- What is your spark now?
- Who helped you develop your sparks?
- As you look back on your life, what advice would you give someone about finding her or his spark?

The Strengths of Your Child's Environment

Even if your teenager doesn't seem to have a spark, you can create a home environment that will encourage and foster the discovery of spark. For some families, that means having a lot of balls (or other types of sporting equipment) around so that kids can easily grab something and start to play. For other families, it means having a stash of art supplies or a library card or a place to putter and dream. Some families have a weekly (or monthly) family time, and they're intentional about creating a variety of meaningful activities to do together, such as volunteering together, playing soccer, doing 3D puzzles, going on hikes in local nature reserves, or going to concerts.

Because many teenagers balk at spending time with their families, encourage each of your children to invite a friend to your family activities. This often gets your teenager to connect with your family (even if it seems a bit peripheral), and you also get to know your teenager's friends more. Some families go bowling, go out for dinner, go mini golfing, check out a teen band that's performing, or attend a school play together. These activities can be free, and they can be extra fun when you widen your family to include one or two of your teenager's friends.

School and Community Leads

Your child's school also is full of possibilities for spark. Which subjects interest your child? Which after- or before-school activities sound interesting? If your teenager is not taking the initiative to get involved, call the school and ask for a list of activities. Sometimes your teenager may not know what's offered, and your help can open up new doors for her.

Also be aware of which teachers and club leaders your teenager is connecting to. Often these individuals know of other opportunities that can enrich (or help discover) your teenager's spark.

Your community often has a number of activities for teenagers, many of which can be hard to find unless you know where to look. Check out your community education catalogue. Is there a class your teenager is interested in—or an activity your family can do together? Find out what your local parks and recreation department, nature center, and community organizations offer. You never know what's out there until you start to look.

NURTURING YOUR TEEN'S SPARKS

As you get to know more about your teenager and explore his rich and complex environments, you'll be more able to help him discover and pursue his spark. Positive human development requires an interplay between a person's emerging capacities and the "soil" in which he is embedded. A rose becomes what it can be when the plant engages an optimal combination of soil, nutrients, water, and oxygen. Similarly, we can see that our teenagers develop best when they are given opportunities to put down their roots and actually change the "soil" in which they are embedded. In spark language, this means being an active participant in finding individuals, programs, and opportunities that bring out their best.

Normal Adolescent Development

Adolescence is one of the most formative periods in the cycle of life. It is a critical time for forming one's identity. It is a time when one begins to create a life narrative, a script that establishes an approach to life. Is my life one of possibility and potential, or is my life destined to be one of drudgery and getting by?

Having sparks and spark champions during adolescence strongly increases the probability that a teen's life script will be built on hope and possibility and potential. Here's why. Sparks provide an anchor for the teen's identity through the empowering discovery that "There are things about me that are good, beautiful, and useful. This is part of me. It is who I am."

The alternative anchors are less savory, but extraordinarily common. The anchor of popularity. The anchor of power. The anchor of status. The anchor of material possessions.

These anchors are not really good anchors. They are external symbols of success that get yanked up in the turbulent whims of public opinion.

One of the adults we interviewed said it eloquently: "The nurturing of sparks in adolescence is so critical, especially today, when so many adolescents are already jaded and bored with life and blind to their own promise. It's important to keep the flame alive—for the individual and for the benefit of society as a whole."

How Sparks Develop in Early Childhood and Middle Childhood

Sometimes sparks have roots that go back to early childhood. A lot of the emphasis in early childhood is on giving young children a variety of activities to explore and experiment with. First-rate child-care centers and preschools have well-defined learning centers and play areas. They schedule daily activities in many areas.

Although a high-quality program can help young children dabble in their sparks, what's key is the adults. Child-care centers and preschools tout low child-to-staff ratios for good reason. The more individual attention that young children get from adults, the more likely they are to thrive. The more that adults introduce children to stimulating activities, the more likely it is that children will discover something that connects with them deep inside.

SPARK TIP
Looking Back—to Look Forward

Because most individuals (especially teenagers) go through periods when they seem not to have a spark, try these ideas to remember sparks from the past. You can do these activities with your teenager's spark in mind, or use them yourself to find your own spark.

- Pull out the baby book (or the baby photo albums). What made the baby smile? Laugh? What were the baby's favorite toys? Interactions?

- Peek back to the preschool years. Again, photo albums, saved art projects, and memories often point to sparks. Preschoolers clearly have strong passions. Some love art and small action figures. Others are riding a two-wheeled bike by age four. Some can spend hours in imaginary play, while others build impressive towers.

- Remember what got your child (or you) excited when she was just a little kid. Those memories often point to spark.

As children grow and enter elementary school, they're exposed to even more activities, topics, and ideas. During the elementary school years, children often play an organized sport, learn a musical instrument, or try some other activity that interests them. Some find their interest early on and build on it, but many continue trying different activities until something catches and grabs them.

If a child has pursued a spark during early and middle childhood, a number of things can happen when he enters the teenage years. He can become even more excited by his interest and begin to master a number of skills. Or he may throw out what interested him before (saying that it is childish or that a parent forced him into it). Some quickly find another spark. Others may appear to be sparkless, instead placing a lot of energy into "not" being who he was and questioning a lot of what he has been raised to believe. This is an important time of searching, but it's also a vulnerable time when kids can fall prey to bad influences, such as substance abuse for thrills.

Then there are teenagers who never had their spark nurtured during childhood. Either they were surrounded by adults who didn't have much interest in them as individuals—or in sparks—or they grew up in chaotic situations that taught them more about surviving than thriving.

Finding Sparks That May Be Hidden

Everyone has a spark. Every child. Every teenager. Every adult. Sometimes it takes a while to explore different places before you can find it. Ideally, we would start children on the spark path from day one, but it is never too late for a person to begin the discovery and development of her spark.

For some young people, the spark is so obvious that it is a matter of affirming what is clearly visible. In Adanna Lewis's case (see Step One), no one needed to name her love of writing. It was there, right in front of her. In other lives, it may take a little patient and knowing probing. I know many teenagers who excel at something they have not put words to. And I often see this unnamed spark when teenagers are interacting informally with their peers.

SPARK STORY
A Father-and-Son Spark Ignition

Dick Hoyt of Holland, Massachusetts, had a son, Rick, who was strangled by the umbilical cord during birth. Rick grew up brain damaged, unable to speak or to control his limbs. Doctors said there was nothing the parents could do.

So Dick and Rick spent time together watching the Boston Bruins. By observing the way Rick's eyes followed the game, Dick began to notice that there was a lot going on in Rick's brain.

Dick convinced some engineers to rig up a computer on which Rick could peck letters by hitting the computer keys with a stick attached to the side of his head. What were Rick's first words? "Go Bruins!"

After that, Rick began communicating a lot more with his parents. During high school, Rick learned about a charity run, and he typed to his dad, "I want to do that."

Dick, who was very out of shape, said that he would help Rick race by pushing him. After the race, Rick typed out, "Dad, when we were running, it felt like I was not disabled anymore."

Spark. There it was. Dick saw it, and he took action.

Dick began training and investigating more races he could push Rick in.

Today they are both adults, and they're still racing together. The two have run in eight-five marathons and competed in 212 triathlons.

What Dick originally thought was Rick's spark also became his own spark. Together, the two of them continue to pursue their shared spark— and give people hope that anyone can have the joy and accomplishment of following his or her spark.

The spark process works for everyone, including kids who are severely wounded—or who have been labeled as hopeless. I recently spent time in Amman, Jordan, with Dr. Curt Rhodes, who is the director of Questscope for Social Development in the Middle East. We visited with street kids who are twelve to thirteen years old and are convinced that they are worthless. Many have been abused in some way: sexually, physically, or emotionally.

One boy, twelve-year-old Ali, was angry because the only person he loved was his grandfather, and Ali's father had murdered him. Questscope matched Ali with Nadia, a young woman studying social work. Over the course of many months, Nadia built a relationship with Ali and taught him how the cycle of violence can stop through restoration and forgiveness. For the first time in Ali's life, he now knows there is an alternative to violence. We need to help young people move from a survival mode to a thriving mode, in which each can name and celebrate his goodness.

BEING PATIENT
DURING DISCOVERY

Some young people discover their spark early in life and stick with it throughout their teenage years, but many go through periods when it seems as if they don't have a spark at all, and might *never* have one. Still others may have had a spark early on but lost it.

Although all these paths are normal, parents can become frustrated when their child has been floundering for a long period of time. But don't let that frustration turn to anger. Take a second and think back about your own journey. When did you first discover *your* spark? What happened along the way? Have you gone through periods when you felt as if you were stuck in neutral?

A young person may go through a seemingly sparkless holding period when she is in the process of discovering—or rediscovering—a spark. Other reasons for such a holding period might include normal childhood development, trauma, and self-consciousness.

Normal Childhood Development

Children's and teenagers' brains and bodies are going through such rapid development that sometimes they put all their energy into one or two aspects of their lives and neglect the rest, including their spark. For example, during puberty, many young teenagers put a lot of energy into their social development. They're on the phone. They're hanging out with their friends. They're on the computer or their cell phones text messaging their friends. They're trying to figure out where they fit in. But while all this social development is going on, their *cognitive* development may slide, which often translates into "forgetting" homework assignments and letting their grades slip. As you can guess, it's essential that you stay involved in your teenager's life, reminding her that all parts are important: friends, family, hobbies, school, and community.

Trauma or Other Major Events

Every once in a while, something may happen that knocks your teen off his path and sets him on a completely new one. For many people, the horror of September 11, 2001, led them to reevaluate their lives and purpose, which affected which spark they pursued and how they developed it. But a life-changing experience doesn't always have to be something that winds up on the nightly news. It could be an accident, the death of a loved one, a grave illness, or some other major life event.

When Kate Atwood was six years old, for example, her mother was diagnosed with cancer. Six years later, when Kate was twelve, her mother died. "I had no idea how much this hurt our family and no idea about how to deal with it," Kate said. First she turned toward sports, activities, and friends, but something was missing.

A trusted friend suggested that Kate spend a week at a bereavement camp in Virginia. At first, Kate rejected the idea. But her friend insisted, and eventually Kate gave in.

The experience changed her life. "I was able to feel and see the benefits of bringing peers together who had shared the experience of losing a loved one," she says. "As I became aware of how important it was to have support—which I didn't have as a child—I realized that my passion in life lies deep in helping others grieving the loss of a loved one."

In 2002, Kate founded Kate's Club, a nonprofit organization that helps kids who are grieving the loss of a parent or sibling. "We all have our challenges," Kate says, "but it is [those] who strive for victories that flourish throughout life."

Self-Consciousness

Even when we are adults, it often takes a lot of courage to do something that no one else is doing. This is even harder for teens.

Because following a spark may mean bucking a trend or standing out in a crowd, some teenagers decide that pursuing a spark is too risky.

For example, teenage boys may think (or be told) that writing poetry or playing the flute is for sissies, even if they'd love to do it themselves. Girls may be accused of not being feminine if they pursue physics or want to play hockey. Be aware of your teenager's interests and how socially acceptable (in her peer group) they are. Reassure your teen and look extra hard for same-sex role models in the same talent area.

In this step, we spent a lot of time getting to know your teen's (and your own) sparks. Doing this is an essential prerequisite for working through the rest of the book. Starting with the next chapter, we'll go deeper with the process of helping your teen ignite his sparks.

Be the Captain of Your Teen's Spark Team

Nobody grasped you by the shoulder while there was still time. Now the clay of which you were shaped has dried and hardened, and nothing in you will ever awaken the sleeping musician, the poet, the astronomer that possibly inhabited you in the beginning.

—Antoine de Saint-Exupéry

Our job as parents is to help our child discover her spark, awaken it, nurture it, celebrate it, make room for it. Our best work as parents is to grasp our child's shoulder while there is still time. We grasp it in order to say, "I believe in you."

YOUR CRITICAL ROLE

Your best role as a parent is to become the captain of your child's spark team. But the team needs to extend out into the community and draw in other champions. A theme that appears over and over in this book is that sparks are only as deep and powerful as the engagement of other key adults who become spark champions in the life of our teens.

The ideal composition of the spark team depends on the nature of the spark. If the spark is artistic in flavor, then the team needs to comprise people who know something about how to nurture this potential. Whether the spark is technical or literary or athletic, a team needs both your orchestration and other caring adults who can help it grow.

Building a team of spark champions means recruiting several adults whom you and your teenager trust and admire. During the teenage years, a teacher, a member of the extended family, a coach, a music teacher, an older sibling, or a college student can have a strong influence on your child. And if your teenager doesn't appear to pay close attention to every word you say, he may be more likely to listen to one of these other adults. That's why it's so important to find other adults to join your child's spark team.

Don't worry: this is not a full-time job. Many family members, mentors, teachers, coaches, and other champions will understand what they need to do and when they need to do it, as a part of their professional and personal activities. Those who don't will quickly learn when you tell them what you want and hope for.

But here's an important point: no matter who is on your child's spark team, *you* need to be the captain. For you, it *is* a full-time job. "The bottom line is that children need to know that they can count on their parents," says Byron Egeland of the Institute of Child Development at the University of Minnesota, who has been conducting a longitudinal study on parents and children since 1975. Even though teenagers are at a stage when they give you the strong impression that they wish you weren't around, it's important for you to be there—and to be involved in their lives.

KEY LESSON 4
Parents Should Be Spark Team Captains

Remember this key research finding: teenagers want their parents to be their spark champions. Does this bear repeating? Yes. Teenagers *want* their parents to be the captain of their spark team. We all need to hear this. And here's another important finding: when we become their spark champions, teens draw closer to us. They come our way. They will start a conversation. And they will listen. Sound like magic? It is.

Why You're So Important in Your Teen's Spark Journey

Kids want and love spark champions. Notice in the stories throughout this book how often moms and dads show up as central to the process of discovering and pursuing a spark. Although being an expert in your child's spark can be helpful, it's far from necessary. What's most important is your *attitude* about your child's spark. You lay the groundwork for a rich, engaged life in the ways that you encourage, advocate, support, and celebrate your child's spark. Without this emotional grounding, it will be much harder for a child to embrace and grow her sparks. Remember: you don't have to be the expert. But you do need to peer into your child's soul and love what you see.

The magic of loving your child's spark reminds me of a favorite saying from Maya Angelou. It goes like this: "Love is knowing a person's song so well that you can hum it back to her on the days she can't remember the melody."

All teenagers will have days, even months, when they forget their song. As a parent, you have no greater role—no greater influence—than to be the voice that reminds a child of her unique, precious song.

You know in all your cells and corpuscles that this is true. Yet it is easy for all of us to lose sight of our powerful capacity to be our child's leading spark champion. We get busy. We may lose sight of our own spark. We develop expectations for our children that may run contrary to their natural sparks. We worry more about competition and financial security than fulfillment. If this happens in your family, you are far from alone.

Our national studies of teenagers tell us four important things about parents:

1. *Teenagers want their parents to be their spark champions.* They want you to cherish them for something that is unique about them and what they bring to the human party. This is what our kids mean when they beseech us to "see me for what I am and not what you want me to be."

2. *When we parents are spark champions, teens are drawn closer to us.* The possibility of communication increases. The possibility that a teen will want to know what we think increases. The possibility that our values will be passed on increases. The possibility that a teen will ask us for advice increases.

3. *Many of us are out of touch with our child's sparks.* One of our studies included 2,015 matched pairs of a parent and a twelve- to seventeen-year-old child. In only 26 percent of these parent-child relationships do parents and teens agree on what the child's sparks are. In another 27 percent of families, the teen names a spark, but the parents don't know it; 16 percent of the time, a parent names a spark, but the child doesn't. And 31 percent of the time, neither parent nor child can identify the spark.

4. *Among young people who have a spark, parents are much more likely to be a spark champion when the child is younger.* Of ten- to twelve-year-olds who have sparks, 91 percent say their parents help them develop their sparks. That number falls to 67 percent of thirteen- to fifteen-year-olds. And then when teens are sixteen to eighteen years old, those with sparks see parents as helpful only 47 percent of the time.

Your teenager may resist your involvement at first. Sometimes you may need to start by being a covert captain of your teenager's spark team. Whether or not your teenager says he wants your input, your involvement is key.

Don't interpret your teenager's resistance as permission to step out of her life. She may just want some space. You may need to step back a little. But never step out. Your involvement is too critical for your teenager's success.

How Teenagers Succeed More When They Don't Go It Alone

People—both teenagers and adults—who have made a significant contribution to their school, work, field of expertise, or society in general will often thank key people who accompanied them on their journey. They often name a parent, a member of their extended family, a teacher, a friend who was instrumental in supporting them. Even teens who grew up under dire circumstances will often point to someone who reached out to them.

For example, my friend and colleague Andy Schneider-Muñoz was the oldest of six kids, and at the age of thirteen, he became the family's mom and dad while his father was serving in the military and his mother was in the hospital for an extended stay. Yet Andy points not to one but to many adults who were willing to help out, including Mr. Sanchez, who would provide transportation in his milk truck, and Mrs. Gomez, who would "lend" Andy extra bread and fruit when the six kids didn't have enough to eat.

Today Andy is an executive of an international nonprofit organization. One of his siblings is the most senior Hispanic executive in a corporation with seventy-eight million customers. Two others are Ivy League–trained doctors. Another is a flight attendant, and the other is a professional horsewoman.

Researchers agree that at least one caring adult can make a difference in a child's life. "The most important finding from our research on kids from a wide variety of backgrounds is that they need a strong sense of caring from at least one competent adult," says Michael Resnick of the University of Minnesota School of Public Health and School of Medicine.

Sure, there are rare examples of young people who flourish even when the adults in their life push them aside. But as a general rule, sparks and attentive adults go hand in hand. In the dynamic interplay of sparks and spark champions, sometimes kids take the initiative to find champions and invite them into their lives. In turn, spark champions guide the expression of the spark or, in some cases, are the critical factor in helping a young person identify her sparks.

CREATING A TEAM OF SPARK CHAMPIONS

Let me say a little more about spark champions. Sparks alone are not enough. The magic is in the combination of sparks *and* multiple spark champions. Spark champions are not just advocates. There's a lot more going on here than first meets the eye.

KEY LESSON 5
Sparks Need Other Champions in Addition to Parents

Yes, parents are important spark champions, but teenagers need more, much more. They need other adults, such as teachers, grandparents, and employers, who help them along their spark journey.

What Spark Champions Do

Every child needs spark champions who

- Affirm the spark

- Encourage its expression

- Model the spark

- Provide opportunities to express it

- Run interference and help eliminate obstacles

- Teach and mentor

- Show up (at recitals, games, performances, play, reading, contests)

The major influence of spark champions during the adolescent years is something deeply transformative, even spiritual. Spark champions give the message—a key life lesson—that there is something within a person that is good, beautiful, and useful to the world. It is a process of revelation at exactly the time that the child's self-identity is being formed.

SPARK TIP
Who Can Be a Spark Champion?

- Mother and father
- Grandparents
- Aunts and uncles
- Siblings
- Cousins
- Rabbis, pastors, imams
- Neighbors
- Peers
- Teachers and other school staff
- Members of your religious community
- Employers
- Coworkers
- Coaches
- Teammates
- Counselors and psychologists
- Youth workers
- Social workers
- Mentors
- Family friends

What Teenagers Think of Spark Champions

So what do America's youth think about spark champions? When they have them, they value them and want even more. When they don't have them, they feel the void. Listen to these voices from our national studies:

> "I am lucky to have a family to help me with my spark. I would love to also find other adults who could help me and believe in me."

> "My mom started me on piano in the first grade and kept me going until my spark set in and it took over on its own. My whole family supports my dream. I also work hard to support my dream. I used my earnings to buy an 88-key digital Roland performance portable piano. I have neighbors who always show up when I perform. And our organist at a local church likes my playing so much he asked me to join him and other adults in playing and practicing together."

> "My parents didn't really help me find my spark, but they have always supported me in whatever I choose to do. When I told them I wanted to run, they were surprised, but they come to all of my races and cheer for me whether it is blistering hot or pouring rain. My coach is very supportive and gives us tips to be better. My teachers are really proud of me and congratulate me when I do good. My mom definitely supports me the most. She has never missed a race of mine, no matter what the weather. She gives me a lot of advice about how to keep my body healthy because she used to work in a hospital. But she can't give me direct advice about running. My coach does, though, because he was a great runner during his high school years."

> "My two favorite teachers are my music teacher and my English teacher. All my teachers are good, but these two are my favorites because they know my spark and keep me on a path to pursue it."

> "My neighbors across the street are like a second family to me. They talk to me about my love of tennis, show up at my matches, and drill with me at the local park."

"My English teachers have always loved my writing spark. They give me extra writing assignments to help develop my skill and are extra hard on grading my assignments to push me to improve. It is something I will never forget about them."

"My friends are very supportive of my comedy, and they are also very honest about my writing and performance. It is something I need because it really helps me grow."

"I'm so into helping other people. My parents give me lots of support, time, and advice. My Girl Scout leader was the one who originally helped me discover my spark. She helped me start countless projects to benefit others. And my Aunt Becky is amazing. She's a great example and mentor. She calls me all the time and gives me advice and support and wonderful ideas on fundraising."

The Ideal Number of Spark Champions

How many spark champions does a young person need? The answer depends on the young person, the contexts she is in, and the nature of the sparks.

There are two general rules or guidelines, however:

1. *The more, the better.* The research is quite clear that sparks shine more brightly when there are multiple spark champions. Two are better than one. Three are even better than two.

2. *The more developmental settings, the better.* We also know that sparks flourish when spark champions are found at home, at school, in youth organizations, in neighborhoods, and in faith communities. To be known for one's sparks in multiple places is a tremendous gift to a young person.

Let's take another look at our national studies of teenagers. Of the teenagers surveyed, 62 percent can clearly identify one or more sparks. Just as important, though, is this question: What percentage of youth have an identified spark *and* three or more spark champions—people who know and support the spark? One without the other is inadequate.

The answer is 37 percent.

This means that 63 percent don't have sparks or don't have adequate spark support. Sad but true. And for my money, this represents a huge loss of creativity, ingenuity, and human capital for the teenagers themselves and for all of us as a society.

The following graph shows the progression of percentages:

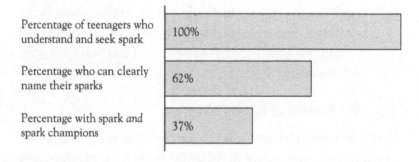

Percentage of teenagers who understand and seek spark	100%
Percentage who can clearly name their sparks	62%
Percentage with spark *and* spark champions	37%

To me, this is a disturbing progression. If we want all our teenagers to thrive, then we want all three of these percentages to be 100. If we were to begin talking more about sparks and becoming spark champions not only for our own teenagers but also for others, imagine how much better this world could be.

Where are the potential sources of spark champions? Besides family, of course, they are in schools, neighborhoods, youth organizations, after-school programs, and congregations. The capacity of each of these settings to generate champions is immense. But when we listen to America's youth, we find that the potential is dormant.

Here are the percentages of youth who say their settings help them develop their spark:

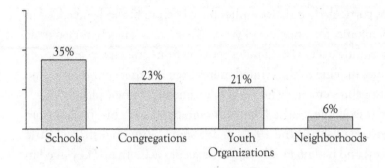

So here is a fact all of us must rally around. The places that our society depends on to nurture our young do not know young people's sparks. If we could change this, the health and vitality of our youth would leap forward.

Peer Champions

One of the biggest sources of spark support could be your teenager's friends (and his classmates). Friends can influence your teenager for the best (and also for the worst). What kind of influence is your teenager experiencing? Ask your teenager these questions:

- Which friends support your spark the most?
- How often do friends talk about their sparks?
- Which friends have a positive impact on your sparks?
- Which friends have a negative impact on your sparks?

Don't overlook what's happening with instant messaging and with Internet postings, such as MySpace. One sophomore, who was proud of the photographs he took at a high school basketball game, posted his best photographs on his MySpace page. The word quickly got out, and soon juniors and seniors were trying to recruit him to take photographs for the school newspaper and yearbook.

Big Brothers Big Sisters

The magic of becoming a healthy and contributing person is about relationship. Some young people have many supporters on which to draw, particularly if their families have been stable and embedded in a community for a number of years. We are now a much more mobile society, however, with families moving from one city to another or families moving to the United States from another country. How do relationships emerge when one is a stranger in a new place?

For example, Sashe Dimitroff emigrated with his mother from Yugoslavia back in the 1970s. They spoke little English, had little money, and had no family support except each other. They lived in a poor neighborhood in Flint, Michigan, where there was a high crime rate.

Understanding the value of an education and strong role models, Sashe's mother enrolled herself in college and enrolled Sashe in the Big Brothers Big Sisters program. Ron Butler, Sashe's Big Brother, was a young man with a family of his own and an active career as a banker. The two of them got together about once a week. Sometimes they would go to a movie or a ball game; other times they would just talk. There were no great speeches, no tests or homework about life lessons. Rather, in the few hours they spent together each week, Ron simply gave Sashe his friendship. Ron also gave Sashe perspective by showing him that the poverty around him, the fights, and the drugs did not have to be part of Sashe's future.

Big Brothers was a great influence at a critical time in Sashe's life. About a decade later, Sashe graduated from the University of Texas with a degree in finance and then moved to New York to work on Wall Street for Merrill Lynch. In 1988 he returned to Texas, enrolled at the University of Houston, and graduated magna cum laude with a law degree and an MBA.

Today Sashe is a partner at a major law firm. He has been married for seventeen years to a wonderful woman who is the love of his life, and they have three beautiful children. Sashe is currently an active member of the board of directors of Big Brothers Big Sisters in Houston.

"It is a success that we broke away from poverty and violence—but I didn't do that by myself," Sashe says. "That success is due to my mother's foresight to leave Yugoslavia because we had no future there, to come to the United States, and to understand the value of an education. My success is due to the constant help we received from Big Brothers Big Sisters."

"Success is not easy—it takes hard work, it takes persistence, and, in the best of all circumstances, it takes relationships. That's my conclusion—that life is all about relationships—the ones that you form and the ones that form you. I feel strongly that Big Brothers Big Sisters helped me personally by giving me tremendous direction and the first, yet most important, tools for a productive future. I wouldn't be here enjoying the blessings of a wonderful family, career, and life without Ron Butler and Big Brothers Big Sisters, and for that I will always be grateful."

Thanking the Other Adults in Your Child's Life

Once you begin thinking about your teen's team of spark champions, you begin to notice and appreciate the efforts of adults who are involved in your teenager's life.

Lynn Stambaugh of Cherry Creek, Colorado, decided to make a list of all the adults who interacted regularly with her four kids, who were nine to fourteen years old. She included teachers, coaches, janitors, bus drivers, music teachers, and neighbors. She was surprised by how long the list was.

She then decided to write each one a letter of thanks. "As an adult working with young people, you play a very important role in the lives of our youth in these 'very hard to grow up' years," she wrote. "You make a difference. Thank you for all your hard work and for your dedication."

Lynn was surprised by the reaction. She received phone calls, e-mails, and thank-you letters. Many of these adults were being intentional about making a difference, but they were rarely recognized—or thanked.

Who are the adults who know your child's name and intentionally greet your child? Who are the spark champions in your child's life?

These are important people. Thank them. Recognize the important work that they're doing. You may be surprised by how a little recognition and gratitude will cement the relationships even further.

SPARK FACT
Disconnected Neighbors

Only 6 percent of teenagers say their neighbors know and nurture their sparks. Isn't that a shame? It's not hard for parents to do something about that. Knock on that door and get better acquainted with everyone in your neighborhood or building. You never know who might be there and how important to you—and your teen—they may become.

Getting Support by Connecting with Other Parents

It's important for teenagers to have a team of spark supporters, but you also need a web of support for yourself. In the past, extended families and neighbors often served this role, but because of today's mobility and the fast pace of our lives, we often find ourselves alone.

A key potential source of support is other parents. Who else understands what you're going through? Other parents can help you find the way—because they're also in the midst of discovering the way themselves.

Even though your life is busy, it's essential to connect with other parents. But how?

Any time you attend a school extracurricular event or some other activity involving your child, talk to at least one other parent. Introduce yourself and learn her name. Strike up a short conversation. Then the next time you see that person, say hello again. Little by little, a relationship will form.

You also can do this while waiting in line for parent-teacher conferences. Middle schools, junior high schools, and senior high schools are famous for setting up conferences where teachers are stationed in a gymnasium or large room, and parents need to wait in long lines to spend a few minutes talking about their children with the teacher. Instead of seeing this as a waste of time (or feeling tempted to skip it all together), think of it as a networking time with parents. Talk with the parents in line. Find out who their teenager is and what they're both into.

As you get to know other parents, find out if they have an e-mail address. Many parents of teenagers are so busy that it's difficult to find time to get together and talk with other parents, but they can stay in touch via e-mail.

Most of all, get to know the parents of your teenager's friends. If you're dropping off your teenager at a friend's home, stop in for a moment to introduce yourself and say hello. If you have time, consider inviting your teenager's friends and their parents over for dessert. Or sit with them at school events.

Creating a supportive network of parents takes time, so be patient. Start slowly and build the network as you can. Sometimes you may need to take a risk, such as calling a parent to ask, "Do you know where Dolores is at this moment?" but that, too, helps to build community.

A WORLD OF SPARKS

A young person can stumble upon a spark (and a spark champion) anywhere. The trick, however, is helping your teenager find these places. Too often, many teenagers try to keep their worlds small. They feel safe within the world they know. As a parent, keep on the lookout for different places where your son or daughter can discover a spark and also find a spark champion.

Where to Find Potential Spark Champions

A spark champion can be anywhere, but teenagers often find their spark champions in specific places. Consider connecting your teenager to one (or more) of these places to see who can become a spark champion for them.

- *Schools*. Check with your school to see which before- and after-school activities are offered. If you have public and private schools in your area, find out what both have to offer. Sometimes you do not need to be a current student to take a one-time evening class or activity. Through these activities, your teenager could find an important spark champion.

- *Community education*. Your community has classes and opportunities for people of all ages. You don't have to be a high school grad to attend these classes, which are often held in local schools and led by people who could become a champion for your teenager.

- *Youth organizations*. Your local YMCA, scouts, 4-H, Boys and Girls Clubs, Camp Fire, Junior Achievement, and other youth organizations offer many activities, events, and camps run by caring, principled adults.

- *Community parks and recreation*. A community parks and recreation department typically offers many opportunities for involvement, and recreational leaders often make a lasting impact on a teenager.

- *Libraries*. Your school, community, and county libraries often will have clubs, classes, and opportunities for teenagers who enjoy connecting with adults with this interest.

- *Camps and retreat centers*. Many have a wide variety of activities, and camp counselors often are significant champions in the lives of teenagers.

- *Businesses and apprenticeships*. Some young people discover and develop their sparks by doing hands-on, experiential activities that are employment and business based. They often grow more when they work with adults who are as excited about business as they are.

- *Traveling and vacations.* Where could you take your teenager that could open up new worlds to her? A family vacation can be a real spark-building experience, and your family could meet someone who makes a strong impression on your teenager.

- *Other important community institutions.* Art museums, zoos, nature centers, historical sites and museums, children's museums, and other organizations often have one-of-a-kind and more unusual offerings that may excite some teenagers and connect them with spark champions.

Centers of Faith

A faith community is one of the important categories of settings where people of many different ages gather and mingle. If you belong to one, this is a great opportunity to get to know young people of different ages and to find out what their spark is.

For example, Aldersgate United Methodist Church in St. Louis Park, Minnesota, publishes an annual June directory of young people with their photographs and their interests and accomplishments. The idea grew out of recognizing the high school and college graduates, until one person said that she wished she knew more about the other kids in the church, too. Thus the directory was born, and it's a hot commodity when it comes out.

The directory highlights awards, accomplishments, and sparks for kids from birth to age twenty-two. The graduating seniors tell about the activities that they were involved with during their senior year and what got them excited about those activities. Write-ups about the younger children tell, for example, about Sam, the four-year-old "who hopped 70 times during his preschool's Hope for Leukemia fundraiser" and about third-grader Erica, who passed American Red Cross Level 5 swimming lessons and loves to read historical novels.

In this same congregation, many individual adults know the children's and teenagers' names, and a number of them have chosen one of the kids to get to know in-depth over the years.

A congregation has multiple opportunities for supporting and deepening a teenager's spark. Many offer programs that promote healthy values and choices. Most have service projects that get teenagers involved in helping others. Many also focus on building caring relationships with teenagers who come through the door. In short, a vital, healthy faith community can be a key place for a teenager to find support for and pursue his spark.

CHARTING A TYPICAL SPARK LANDSCAPE

Once you begin identifying the people and places that have a positive influence on your teenager's spark, it's often helpful to take a broader view and to chart your teen's spark landscape.

For example, Taneesha Saresh is a sixteen-year-old living in upstate New York. She comes from a family of relatively modest means. Her mom provides day care for four children in their home. Her father is a police officer. She has an older brother, who is a freshman at a state university, and a younger sister.

When Taneesha was little, her parents remember how she used the back porch as a stage. She'd create plays and put on costumes to act out the parts. She'd use a stick or a spoon as a microphone. In middle school, it became obvious to Mrs. Garcia, her music teacher, that Taneesha needed an outlet for her acting spark. Because the middle school had no drama program, Mrs. Garcia hooked her up with a community theater. On three occasions, when she was thirteen and fourteen, she got bit parts in plays.

Taneesha says that the person who inspires her the most is her mother. "She always tells me that I can achieve whatever I want to and that I should let nothing get in my way. She tells me that she let other people rule her life so she never pursued her life dream to be an artist." Although Taneesha's mom has no particular expertise in acting or drama, she provided two critical spark-generating resources: constant encouragement and access to drama experiences. She took Taneesha to numerous high school and community college plays. Dad never says much, according to Taneesha, but he is also very supportive of her spark. When she was fifteen, Mom, Dad, Taneesha, and her younger sister took a train into New York City to see two Broadway plays.

When Taneesha entered high school, the opportunities started to expand. A high school drama coach gave Taneesha coaching and guidance. Three teachers learned of her passion and initiated meaningful conversations with her about the world of drama and acting. Sometimes they shared reviews of plays from newspapers and news magazines. It strikes Taneesha as very "cool" that these three teachers stayed in her life even though she no longer has any classes with them.

A guidance counselor at school supplied Taneesha with names of colleges that have strong performing arts programs. And last summer, her drama teacher connected her with a summer job at the local YMCA to help teach acting to younger children. There she met two staff members who have become major champions for her and attend her high school plays.

When we chart Taneesha's spark landscape, it looks like Figure 4.1.

When I asked Taneesha about what difference her spark and spark champions have made in her life, she said that her champions have helped her believe in herself and have provided the support she needs to focus on learning all she can. She also has deepened her aspiration to make acting her life work. But she knows she needs to knuckle down and develop a resume and an application that will get her into a good college. She looks back on her adolescent years with gratitude for the people and places that nurtured her. And let's not underestimate the YMCA experience of teaching acting to younger children. This opportunity to give back may, in the long run, open Taneesha's imagination to a life of teaching and mentoring.

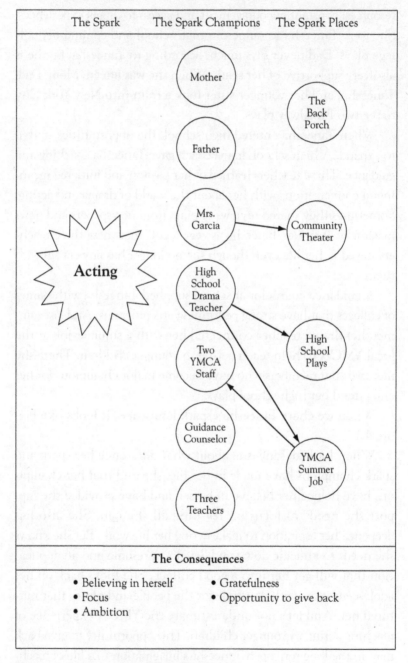

The Spark   The Spark Champions   The Spark Places

Mother

The Back Porch

Father

Mrs. Garcia → Community Theater

Acting

High School Drama Teacher → High School Plays

Two YMCA Staff

Guidance Counselor

YMCA Summer Job

Three Teachers

The Consequences

- Believing in herself
- Focus
- Ambition
- Gratefulness
- Opportunity to give back

Figure 4.1: Taneesha's Spark Landscape

In charting a spark landscape, it's good to keep track of these consequences. I see three things in Taneesha's story that are priceless and likely to inform the rest of her life: she is believing in herself, recognizing and expressing gratitude, and learning how her sparks can be useful to the world.

Relationships with caring and principled adults are the conduits through which a young person observes values in action. They are the conduits that transfer human wisdom. They are the portals to a responsible and engaged future. They are spark champions. It's hard to imagine a more powerful human experience than to have adults who know a child so well that they can hum back her song "on the days she can't remember the melody."

As the captain of your teen's spark team, it's essential to remember your role and to stay in the game. Even when you find other important spark champions for your teenager, your teenager still needs you, which is why your role is critical.

Your role also plays an important part in Step Five, keeping your teen's spark lit. There will be days when your teenager will experience ups and downs in his spark journey, times of doubts or frustration, times of uncertainties and changing feelings. When you're there for your teenager unconditionally, you can help him find the way back and keep the spark ignited.

STEP FIVE

Keep Your Teen's Spark Lit

Keeping a spark going isn't always an easy, step-by-step process. Teenagers with multiple sparks may sometimes find themselves dabbling in five things at once. Those with a single spark may find they bounce around from action to action. Some will encounter periods when they feel that they have lost their spark completely.

School counselors often express frustration with helping young people keep their spark lit and plan for their future. Many teenagers get distracted by other things, such as dreaming of becoming professional athletes or playing in an all-star rock band. Counselors know that only a few will actually break into these highly competitive fields and even fewer will do so for a long period of time.

Yet we can nudge teenagers to explore beyond the glittering distractions that are often more about fame and fortune than about connecting with the deepest part inside them. We can help them keep their true spark lit, the spark that is connected to their being, rather than something they believe would be most glamorous in our society.

CREATE A SPARK-SUPPORTING CULTURE

Our American culture doesn't always support the sparks of our teenagers.

This was Terri's experience. She knew her spark: she wanted to create, design, and build Web sites. She saw how the school had hired a professional and created a highly functional and beautiful Web site, and she wanted to learn to do it herself. She became passionate about Web sites, read everything she could about them, and even got a part-time job at a computer store where she could be around people who knew a lot more about the subject than she did.

The problem, however, was that she received no support for or guidance about her spark. She knew she needed experience and exposure to learn more about designing and building Web sites. But there was no support at home or school to get this kind of education, no special classes at school, no parents who were interested in helping her learn more about the field or who could pay for the specialized training required. Then she let her homework slip so that she could work more hours in order to buy more computer software. After graduating from high school, she had no support for going to college or getting any more knowledge through training. Many of her friends went on to college while Terri worked full-time, at minimum wage, for the computer store.

"I'm working forty hours a week now but not really learning enough yet to break into the field," she says.

Being able to name your authentic spark is one thing. But the spark can fade and go out without the support that's required to deepen and cultivate it. As a parent, you can do a lot in this area.

Cultivate Your Teen's Spark

Too many think that a spark will flourish on its own, but in order for a spark to ignite and hold a flame, it needs a number of things:

> A *place to grow.* Look at your home. Does your teenager have a place to work on his spark? What about other places: a sports field, a band room, a special class, or an art studio?

Time to grow. Musicians master their instruments by practicing. Athletes develop their skills by working out, doing drills, and practicing. Teenagers need time to focus on their spark and develop it.

Discipline to grow. It takes discipline to deepen a spark. Help your teenager develop the discipline to focus on her spark— every day (or as many days a week as possible). She won't get anywhere by playing around with her spark once in a while or only when she feels like it.

People to encourage the growth. How do you encourage your teenager's spark? Who else helps your teenager with her spark? Assist your teenager in finding people who will help her go deeper.

Don't do this alone. Find others to support you and your teenager along the spark journey. A great place to start is to create a network of parents who will join you in discussing sparks and how to support them. Think of it as a spark support group.

SPARK TIP
Starting a Spark Support Group

Photocopy the pages in Step Three that ask these three questions: (1) What are your child's current or potential sparks? (2) When did you first understand about or see these sparks? Are they new, or did they show up earlier? When? (3) Who are the adults who know and support your teenager's spark? What do they do to help the spark shine?

My publisher has a better idea—buy a few copies of this book and give them to your friends. In either case, I think you'll find that discussing the three questions with other parents will be one of the best conversations you'll ever have about parenting. All you need to do is set up the conversation with a couple of other parents by explaining the definition of sparks and why they matter. Then pass out the questions. Let folks spend five minutes recording their answers. Then start talking.

Here's what will happen. First, you'll start to see your friends' children through a spark lens. Second, you'll get all kinds of insights about how to be a spark champion. The result could well be your finding more spark champions for your teenager and your becoming a spark champion for other parents' teenagers too.

I would love to hear your stories about these conversations with your friends. How did they go? What new ideas did you learn? How are adults relating to teens differently? Post your comments at www.ignitesparks.com.

Talk About Sparks in Effective Ways

A key way to create a spark-supporting culture for your teenager is to start conversations about spark. But how do you talk to your teenager when your teenager doesn't want to talk to you? Many teenagers go through phases when they don't want to be seen with their parents, let alone talk to them. Yet it's important to keep initiating conversations with them, because they're still listening, even if they don't act as if they are.

Remember the idea I mentioned in Step Three about talking to your teenager while driving in a car (or riding a bus or subway)? I believe it's important to raise it again. Teenagers have a hard time talking with their parents when they're face-to-face. If you can find a way to be shoulder to shoulder or side by side (such as riding in a car or doing a family chore together), you're more likely to be able to talk.

One dad had a daughter who stopped talking to him for two years. Every night, he would check in with her before bed, and he would ask her about her day. She wouldn't say a word. He then would tell her briefly about his day and told her that he was thinking of her. Some days, he told her how proud he was of her, even though he wasn't proud of their relationship.

Years later, the daughter told her dad, "Remember all those great talks we had late at night when I was in junior high? Those were my favorite times."

His daughter hadn't said a word! He was the one who had done all the talking, but she was listening. She was paying attention to how he was treating her—even though she was oblivious to how she was treating him.

Consider asking your teenager these questions to get the conversation started about her spark:

- What special talent or interest do you have that gives you joy and energy?

- Who encourages you to do these things?

- What squashes your enthusiasm?

- How do you deal with the barriers that get in your way?

- How long have you been following this special talent or interest?

- Which adult role models do you have whose spark is like yours?

- How does your spark give your life meaning?

- Where do you hope your spark will lead you?

Let's hope that your initial conversation about sparks is only the start of many conversations to come. For sparks to thrive, you will want to establish some pattern in keeping the dialogue going. I know parents and teens who carve out an hour a week in a coffee shop, on the porch, or at the kitchen table—to check in with each other on their spark experiences. These are not conversations about obligations, rules, or responsibilities. Instead, they are conversations about possibility, passion, and purpose. It's important to keep the tone upbeat. And it's important to listen.

Notice when your teenager comes to life because of his spark. Say, "I love seeing you like this!" Make the connection between your child's joy and his spark process. That's the big lesson that adults are being taught at age fifty: pursuing your spark brings your life great joy. It's important that this lesson sink into the marrow of each child—long before he becomes an adult.

SPARK TIP
Mealtime Magic

Research reveals that eating together as a family is important glue that holds families together. The next time you eat together, try these ideas to make your mealtime even more meaningful:

- *Take turns telling each other* about your day at work or home, and especially what's currently happening on your own personal spark journey.

- *Laugh* about the funny things that have happened to you on your spark journey.

- *Explain what inspires you* and why.

- *Ask questions* to learn more about each other's spark.

- *Enjoy being together* as a family.

As the captain of your teenager's spark team, help your teenager see the connection between his spark and his authentic self. For example, talk about questions such as these:

- How does your spark express your true self?

- How does your spark give your life meaning?

- How does your spark make life better for other people or for the world?

- How do you feel about yourself when you're following your spark?

- How does your spark impact how you feel about your future?

HELP YOUR TEEN BUILD A SPARK PLAN

Even if your teenager knows her spark and is exploring it, she won't get far without a plan. Because of the world of technology that teenagers live in, planning ahead further than two minutes can be hard for a lot of teenagers. They're used to getting instant answers to their instant questions. If they're stumped, they text message or call someone on their cell phones and find out what to do next. They're impulsive and fast acting, and they expect immediate results.

Yet your teenager's spark won't develop without his setting (and meeting) some goals. "Being busy does not always mean real work," said the inventor Thomas Edison. "There must be forethought, system, planning, intelligence, and honest purpose, as well as perspiration. Seeming to do is not doing."

Focusing on Your Teen in Building the Plan

The spark plan needs to come from your teenager, not from you. But there are questions you can ask that will help your teenager create a plan. Consider starting with the five key questions shown in Table 5.1.

As we've discussed earlier in the book, our teens are not getting enough support for their sparks. Too many youth move through adolescence without meaningful and sustained relationships with caring and principled adults. Sure, kids know adults. They are

Table 5.1

Questions	Ideas for Action
1. What more can I do to help you with your spark?	
2. Who else could be a spark champion for you? What do you wish each person would do?	
3. Which places or programs would help your spark grow?	
4. How can we create the ideal weekly schedule to help foster your spark?	
5. What else would help your spark?	

called teachers and neighbors and employers and coaches. But for many, these are superficial relationships without the depth needed for the adult to know and nourish what makes a young person shine.

According to Search Institute's ongoing studies of youth, only 43 percent receive support and encouragement from three or more nonparent adults. No wonder, then, that when we poll teenagers about adults who know them well enough to see and nourish their sparks, we see only a minority reporting that they have three or more spark champions.

SPARK FACT

The Disturbing Lack of Adult Relationships

The percentages of youth who report that they have supportive and encouraging relationships with three or more adults are far too low during the teenage years.

Grade	Youth with Three or More Adult Relationships (%)
6	46
7	43
8	42
9	42
10	42
11	44
12	45

The Importance of Relationships

Imagine the capacity to nourish sparks that are locked up and frozen in our schools, neighborhoods, youth organizations, and congregations. America's youth tell us how rare it is for these settings to have spark champions. Remember the numbers from Step Four. In our national polls, only 35 percent of youth say schools help them develop their sparks; 23 percent see congregations as helpful; 21 percent are nourished by youth organizations; and a paltry 6 percent find spark nourishment in their neighborhoods.

If only the adults in the places where our kids spend time could awaken to the power of knowing and nurturing sparks. As the captain of your teen's spark team, you can have a dramatic impact by helping the adults in your child's life see your child through a spark lens. Think of it as rallying the troops around your teenager. And as you call forth the spark-nurturing energy for your child, you might light a fire that spreads the idea of spark to *all* youth.

SPARK TIP
Awakening Spark Relationships

Try these ideas to encourage other adults in your teenager's life to become spark champions:

At School

- Ask for a parent-teacher conference with your teenager's favorite teacher and discuss your child's spark.

- When you hear about a teacher making a difference in your teenager's life, drop her a note and say how much you appreciate it.

- If you're willing and able to invest more time, join the parent-teacher organization. Once you know people, bring up the idea of sparks for the group to focus on.

In Your Neighborhood

- Attend National Night Out (the first Tuesday of August each year) and meet your neighbors. Introduce them to your teenager.

- Get to know your neighbors' names. Find out what interests them and see if there are any spark connections between your teenager and a neighbor.

- Organize an informal activity (such as a pickup basketball game or making cookies together) for young people in your neighborhood.

In Your Faith Community

- Attend intergenerational activities and help your teenager get to know people of different ages in your congregation.

- Get to know other teenagers in your congregation. Find out what their spark is. Encourage your teenager and other teenagers to pursue their sparks.

- Find adults who have the same interest as your teenager. For example, if your teenager enjoys music, connect him to adult musicians. If your teenager is into technology, introduce him to a soundboard operator or videographer.

New Ways of Planning Spark Support

A simple action by a significant adult can get your teenager thinking and following a spark in a new way. For example, each year for Christmas, Nathan Dungan of Minneapolis gives cash to his niece, Kelly, age sixteen, and his nephew, Peter, thirteen. But the gift has a catch.

Nathan gives Kelly and Peter three checks each—one to give away to charity, one to save, and one to spend any way they want. It's Nathan's way of encouraging Kelly and Peter to think about their money in three ways: to share, to save, and to spend. "Kids need help forming values about money," Nathan says, "especially in today's world where they're constantly bombarded by messages telling them to buy, buy, buy."

For Kelly, the gift has ignited a spark inside her. "It makes me feel good when I can share money to help other people," she says about the gift from her uncle. It's worth remembering for all of us that when we offer young people new experiences, along with good guidance, we may also be helping them discover a new spark.

KEY LESSON 6
Great Things Happen When Kids Pursue Their Sparks

School grades rise. Depression decreases. Violence drops. Physical health improves. Hope and purpose rise. In studies of more than three thousand young people, we find strong scientific evidence for positive impact. A lot of great things happen when kids pursue their sparks.

Support from Schools

There's a particularly important lesson for schools in our spark research. Of all the positive consequences that come to youth when they pursue their sparks and have several spark champions on their team, the one that rises to the top is school performance. Both grades and school attendance increase significantly when youth thrive.

Hence, promoting school achievement is not just about the rigor of the curriculum, classroom size, or per-pupil expenditures. As much or more, school achievement stems from the way spark-nurturing relationships occur in the classroom, the hallways, and in the locker rooms. Knowing and nourishing sparks is an academic achievement strategy that needs to rise to the top in all of America's schools.

HELP YOUR TEENAGERS ASSESS THEIR JOURNEY SO FAR

Knowing your spark is a critical step in leading a thriving life. But how your teenager puts her spark into play in the world, and how well she mobilizes people and settings to know, affirm, and use her spark are also critical features in living a thriving life.

Journal Writing

One way to do this is to encourage your teenager to keep a journal (diary or scrapbook) of the ways she explores her spark. What could she include?

- A list of activities your teenager does to deepen the spark

- Goals your teenager has set and deadlines for meeting goals

- Important people who support your teen's spark (and examples of how they help)

- Helpful Web sites

- Other resources

This journal becomes the story of your child's passion in life and passion for life. It also can serve as an inspiration when your teenager hits obstacles.

Your teenager also can take the following questionnaire. Encourage him to complete it as honestly as he can. (And if you're on the spark journey as well, go ahead and take it yourself.)

Keeping the Spark Lit Self-Assessment

Part I: Support for Sparks

1. I have people in my life who see and appreciate my sparks.
   a. Very true (3)
   b. Somewhat true (2)
   c. Not true (1)

2. My community provides many opportunities for me to express my spark.
   a. Very true (3)
   b. Somewhat true (2)
   c. Not true (1)

3. People often ask me to do things that help me use my spark.
   a. Very true (3)
   b. Somewhat true (2)
   c. Not true (1)

Add up your part I points here: ____

Part II: Actions I Take

1. I make my sparks a priority in my life.

    a. Very true (3)

    b. Somewhat true (2)

    c. Not true (1)

2. I am purposeful in finding time and opportunities to express my spark.

    a. Very true (3)

    b. Somewhat true (2)

    c. Not true (1)

3. I seek people who share my spark.

    a. Very true (3)

    b. Somewhat true (2)

    c. Not true (1)

Add up your part II points here: ____
Add together your points from parts I and II: ____ (A)

Part III: Obstacles

1. I have people in my life who don't want me to use or express my spark.

    a. Very true (3)

    b. Somewhat true (2)

    c. Not true (1)

2. I believe that the best time to find spark is sometime in the future when I have more time and fewer obligations.

    a. Very true (3)

    b. Somewhat true (2)

    c. Not true (1)

3. I am just too busy to focus on my sparks.

   a. Very true (3)

   b. Somewhat true (2)

   c. Not true (1)

   Add up your part III points here: ____ (B)
   Subtract B from A. This is your thriving score: ____

Understanding Your Thriving Score:

13–15 points: Kudos. Your spark shines in your life and in the world. You're putting your spark into play in a meaningful way. Keep going. The world is better because of you.

10–12 points: On a hopeful path. Your life is full of possibilities. Try to be more purposeful about the choices you make. This may mean finding additional spark champions in your life and making more time and opportunity to express that which gives you joy.

7–9 points: What is in your way? As a teen or a parent, you can get pulled in many directions. If you feel too fragmented, you can end up living a life of more frustration than meaning. If you know your spark clearly, you can work at expressing it more.

6 points or less: Time for a life checkup. If you are unclear about your spark, talk with your closest soul mates to help you identify what is good and beautiful and useful about you. Hear it. Affirm it. Then create a plan, beginning with small steps, to put your spark into play.

THE IMPORTANCE OF DISCIPLINE

Discipline is crucial to keeping your teenager's spark alive. Following one's spark is not only about joy; it also requires dedication and work.

The teenagers who understand this can go far with their spark. They make personal sacrifices in its pursuit. Maybe they practice shooting baskets from all angles. Or they play an instrument on most days (and for a lot longer than five minutes). Developing the discipline takes time, and it's not easy in this culture that emphasizes immediate gratification and instant results.

Perseverance

At the core of self-discipline is the concept of perseverance. It means to keep trying when things are difficult and to bring one's best efforts to each task. And many of a parent's opportunities to teach about perseverance arise in relation to a child's spark.

When your teenager is inspired to try a musical instrument or a new sport, you can help him set goals for learning and staying focused. Imagine together how far he might be able to go with this spark if he practices each day and strives always to do his best.

As a parent, you can watch for opportunities to model and teach about these useful concepts:

- Not giving up when things are difficult

- Striving for excellence, not perfection

- Getting perspective by thinking of the long term or the big picture

- Learning from our mistakes or failures

- Taking actions, even small ones, rather than procrastinating

You can watch for opportunities during the common, daily events of life as well, from making the bed each morning to doing homework each evening.

Homework

Kids often complain about doing homework, yet completing homework every evening teaches kids important skills about planning, decision making, and follow-through. In a Search Institute study of more than three million young people, researchers found that girls are more likely to do homework (53 percent) than boys (40 percent).

Teach your teenager about the power of homework and how it affects his grades in school. Insist that he spend time each day doing homework. If your teenager doesn't have homework on a particular school night, encourage him to read or do some other educational activity to get in the habit of doing homework every night.

Your teenager may attempt to point out that homework has nothing to do with his spark. "I want to be an artist. Why do I need to study math?" he may ask.

So be sure to point out that math clearly has relevance to art. For example, such artists as M. C. Escher, Leonardo de Vinci, and Albrecht Dürer used mathematical thinking to create their art. If that doesn't convince your child (especially if he admires the artist Jackson Pollock, who created artworks by flinging paint at a canvas), make the case that we need to be well-rounded individuals and that your child's learning academic subjects teaches him about planning, critical thinking, abstract thinking, goal setting, and many other skills that are essential for *any* spark.

Don't let your teenagers off the hook in terms of academics, even when classes and assignments get hard. Don't let them use their spark as an excuse to slack off at school.

"Children are far more competent at early ages than adults in our society give them credit for," writes William Damon in *Greater Expectations*. "They thrive on challenges and on chances to prove themselves. Competence motivation is a natural part of every child's repertoire. If encouraged, it enables children to develop their capacities with zest and vigor."

YOU'RE ALWAYS A ROLE MODEL

Every day, your teenager is watching you. Listening to you. Paying attention to what you do. What kind of example are you setting in terms of spark?

A great role model is not a perfect person. A great role model is human. Great role models do their best, but they also admit their mistakes. They talk about their experiences. They learn and grow— and in the process, show what it's like to pursue a spark and live a meaningful life.

If you are on the path of pursuing your own personal spark, you need not only to model it but also to talk about it. What do you talk about—especially if your spark isn't something that gets your teenager excited? Talk about the process. Discuss key people who inspire you and keep you going. Bring up turning points that pulled you out of a slump. Your teenager can relate to your process, even if you and she have radically different sparks.

The Passion of Your Spark

How do you know when someone is passionate about something? He's excited about what he does. He tells others about it.

For example, even though Fred was a computer engineer by day, he loved playing the tuba. In the evening, he would play songs for his two daughters. When they were young, he would play "Twinkle, Twinkle Little Star" and other preschooler hits. As they became teenagers, he sometimes played their favorite Beatles song. Even though they teased their dad about always lugging around a big hunk of metal, the daughters knew their dad was passionate about the tuba. Seeing his passion made it easier for them to find their spark.

The Joy of Your Spark

Your teenager may not understand why you love working as a plumber, but she recognizes joy and happiness. One plumber says that he enjoys pointing out to his teenagers all the homes and businesses in his community that he's helped. "Plus, I get to do something different every day," he tells them. "And people are always happy when I finish because I solve their plumbing problems." Talk about what lights your fire and how following your spark brings you joy.

The Energy of Your Spark

A true spark gives you energy. It's something that you want to do, something you find yourself motivated to do. Talk about this energy. Contrast it with some of the activities that you're obligated to do but don't like to do (such as dusting or taking out the garbage). Model how it's important to find a spark that gives you energy not only for pursuing it but also for doing other things. Talk about how much easier it is to take out the garbage—and fulfill your other responsibilities—if you spend most of your time doing something you enjoy.

The Gratitude for Your Spark

A true spark is a gift. Talk about it that way. Too many adults see work and life as drudgery. (That means they're not pursuing their spark.) Instead, pursue your spark. Keep the flame going. Be an adult who is grateful for your spark and how it enriches your life. Express how thankful you are that you have the spark that you have.

YOUR SPARK JOURNEY

Unfortunately, adults tend to talk more when life is not going well. We complain. We grumble. We point out the injustices, and as we do so, our kids soak up what to do when the spark journey gets difficult: complain and grumble.

What if we as parents became more intentional about talking about our spark journeys when they are going well? What could we model and teach our kids about following their sparks?

SPARK FACT

Who Is the Number-One Role Model of Teenagers?

When teenagers were asked who society's most important role models are today, 68 percent of them said their parents, which ranked number one. When choosing role models, teenagers said they look to people who have these principles: honesty, integrity, loyalty, and truthfulness.

Sometimes the tables are turned, and a child or a teenager can have a big impact on a parent's spark. Each person's spark journey looks more like a labyrinth than a set of steps. We have high points and low points. We revisit certain steps and wonder if we're going in circles or if we're going deeper to a new level. Sometimes your teenager can be making progress while you, like Jeanne, feel stalled out.

Jeanne had always made jewelry, but for the past few years all the light from her spark had gone out. Jeanne's father had been ill with cancer, and that had taken a lot of her energy. Jeanne still designed jewelry, but her designs felt flat and ordinary. No matter what she tried, she just couldn't get inspired. It didn't help that she was exhausted from the caregiving for her father and being a parent of a teenager.

Jeanne's daughter, Keesha, had stumbled upon her own spark around the same time that her mother had lost hers. Keesha had tried out for a school play and had gotten a part. Now, two years later, Keesha was an understudy at the children's theater, and she was passionate about acting.

Jeanne attended Keesha's performances, but it wasn't until Keesha was in the play *Pinocchio* that Jeanne realized something about herself. She had become like the puppet, her strings being pulled by her father's illness. Jeanne had stopped having lunch with one of her best friends because she felt crunched for time and embarrassed that all she had to talk about was the stress in her life. Jeanne marveled at how Keesha's light shone through in the performance, even though Keesha and her boyfriend had recently broken up. Jeanne knew she needed to become "real" again—just like her daughter. And after that performance, she started making jewelry again.

The tide can also turn when you and your teenager are struggling with your sparks at the same time. When Gary's son, Rob, wanted to drop out of high school, Rob's desire to quit resurrected a deep pain in Gary, because Gary had dropped out of high school to support his family when Gary's father died and his mother became ill.

So Gary made a deal with Rob. If Rob agreed to stay in high school, Gary would go back and complete the degree he had once abandoned. They could study together—and graduate together.

Both father and son worked toward their diploma, and in 1997, they both graduated from Marshall High School in Marshall, Minnesota. Together they helped light each other's spark—and keep it lit.

HELP YOUR TEEN OVERCOME OBSTACLES

As I said, the spark path can be a labyrinth; it doesn't usually go straight up with each step higher and better than the step before. Sometimes your teenager will find himself going through difficulty, and it's easy for him to lose his way.

Setbacks

If your teenager is pursuing a spark, he will encounter setbacks (if he hasn't already). What do you do when your child finds himself in this situation? It depends on what the rough patch is about. Ask your teenager these questions:

- What is the difficulty? Or is it a sense that something isn't right and you don't know what it is yet?

- Is this a short-term difficulty that will blow over if you make a few adjustments? If so, what changes do you need to make?

- What can you control? What is out of your control?

- Do you need to change your setting or the people you're with?

- Is this about boredom? Or are you sensing that you're in over your head?

Dig deeper into the obstacle. Typically, the obstacles that may arise in your teenager's spark journey fall into one of these major types.

Others Discourage Your Teenager

Your teenager prepares and prepares for a piano recital or to try out for the tennis team, and an admired adult is downright mean: "You won't make it. You're not good enough." Or even worse, an adult or a peer shames your child: "Why are you even here? Why do you think *you* can play the piano?"

These harsh reactions can crush your teenager's spirit and squelch her spark (or send it deep into hiding). Many individuals who have followed their spark over a course of several years will often talk about one (or more) individuals who tried to talk them out of their spark—or worse, made fun of their spark or wounded them emotionally.

Ask your teenager questions such as these:

- Why do you think this person had such a strong reaction to your spark?

- Do you agree with this person's assessment? Why or why not?

- What if the person was having a bad day and took it out on you?

- How can you recover from this blow?

- How can you become more comfortable with your spark—no matter how others criticize it?

- How can you move forward?

Your Teenager Gets Ill or Has an Accident

Accidents happen. So do illnesses. Justin, a teenage soccer player, was thrilled to make the varsity team as a freshman. Then, during the first game, Justin got hit hard, and his collarbone was broken. He was out for the rest of the season.

Justin worked hard to recover, and on the first day of practice as a sophomore, he was ready to play and have a better season. But Justin got hit again and was injured for the rest of the season. Two years of injuries.

Most teenagers would have taken the injuries as a sign to do something else and would have quit, but Justin's family taught him that setbacks are part of the spark journey. Justin worked through the setbacks and started on the varsity team as a junior. He made it through the season without injury, and his team won the division title.

A Spark Goes Dark

As kids move from childhood into the teenage years, their spark may seem to disappear. A lot of young teenagers become more interested in passive activities than in active ones. Many like watching TV, talking on the phone, playing video games, spending time on the computer, or just hanging out with their friends. A lot of kids drop the childhood activities at which they actually excelled.

Marian Diamond, PhD, the author of *Magic Trees of the Mind*, contends that the teenage years are the years when many teenagers "uproot the trees that their parents planted during childhood." This is a result of the massive changes going on in the teenage brain and of the teenager's efforts to form an identity separate from her parents.

Diamond recommends that parents should not remain passive and should instead encourage their teenagers "to plant new trees." How? By introducing them to new, stimulating activities. Connect your teenagers to interesting, caring adults. Help them discover academic subjects or hobbies that excite them, or a new way of practicing a former spark. In essence, parents can introduce their teenagers to new spark possibilities until they find one (or more) that resonates with who they are.

Your Teenager Wants to Quit

Parents often feel alarmed when their young teenager stops playing the violin or trumpet after three to five years. Or the child may quit playing basketball or soccer after years of playing on a team. Some parents watch their young teenagers drop everything and then replace these worthwhile childhood activities with chasing the opposite sex, going to the mall, or playing paintball in the backyard or at a nearby park.

If your teenager is in the "dropping out of everything" mode, place some boundaries on what he's doing. For example, one parent was not happy when her son Micah decided to quit the viola after five years of private lessons. He had excelled at the instrument and had even earned a spot on a regional youth symphony. Micah, however, was insistent. The viola no longer excited him. He refused to practice. His private teacher said she would no longer teach him, and Micah happily agreed.

The parents, however, didn't agree with Micah—or his music teacher. Micah's mother said, "If you want to quit the viola, that's your choice, but you have to choose another instrument. You need to take private lessons and practice."

At first, Micah resisted, but his parents were insistent. Micah wasn't allowed to run with his friends until he had chosen an instrument that "he was excited about."

At first, Micah complained to his friends. How could his parents do this to him? It wasn't fair to force this on him!

As it turned out, most of Micah's friends were in a similar situation. They, too, no longer liked the musical instruments they had chosen as nine- and ten-year-olds. They wanted to quit, but their parents were asking, "What instead?"

So the boys began talking about the music and the instruments that excited them. One switched from classical piano to jazz piano played on an electric keyboard. Another switched from the flute to the electric guitar. Another went to the electric bass. And Micah? Percussion. He wanted a drum set.

Again, Micah's parents were firm. They would buy him a drum set only after he had taken six months of lessons on a practice pad. They weren't going to invest a lot in something that could possibly change within a few months. They had seen other teenagers go through phases where they were excited about one thing for three to six months and then switched to something completely different.

Six months later, percussion lessons were going well. Micah got a drum set, and the boys began forming a band.

What a Caring Adult Can Do

Some teenagers have involved parents who are willing (and able) to invest time, energy, and even money in discovering, pursuing, and deepening their spark. But what about teenagers who don't? Can they discover their spark?

The answer is yes.

All it takes is a caring adult.

I hear countless stories of disadvantaged teenagers finding a spark by getting to know an adult who is willing to invest her time with the teenager. The challenge, however, is that disadvantaged teenagers often have a lot of issues to work through. If you are in the role of caring adult, be patient. Be persistent. Be a positive force, but also be respectful of the teenager's journey. Some will surprise you by turning their lives around. Others will disappoint, but *never* give up on them.

Kareem Moody works with teenagers who are in danger of dropping out of school, and he advises parents, "Help yourself by asking for help from other adults when you need it. Remember, you don't have to do all the work of building relationships with kids on your own." Again, this speaks to the power of a team of spark champions for *every* teenager.

KEY LESSON 7
Most Teens Don't Have Enough Spark Champions in Their Lives

It's important to keep mobilizing adults to be involved with our teenagers' sparks. Teenagers need adults to help them not only discover their sparks but also pursue and deepen their sparks. Spark + support = success.

Trusting Your Child's Instinct for Her Right Spark

If your teenager has a spark for something that worries you or doesn't interest you in the least, you're not alone. Teenagers often find sparks that their parents find downright puzzling (or even annoying).

One parent became alarmed with her thirteen-year-old daughter, Liza, when Liza's grades began to slide and she became most interested in covering her body with tattoo-like drawings with permanent marker. The mom first tried to find out what was going on with the girl, but Liza refused to speak with her. Liza was mad, but she wouldn't tell her mom why. Liza's dad took her out for lunch a few times and made her laugh, but that was as far as he could get.

So the parents confided their difficulty to one of Liza's favorite aunts. They told her they were worried and that they didn't know what to do. So the aunt invited Liza to the girl's favorite pizza parlor and went bowling with her, which is what Liza loved to do. As they had fun together, Liza gradually confided that her best friend was cutting herself (using a razor blade to make herself bleed) and that she was worried about her. The problem, however, was that whenever she and the friend talked, her friend made a lot of sense. Kids were mean at the junior high. They stole each other's things. They vandalized lockers. They ruthlessly harassed each other. Liza hated school. She hated what was happening to her best friend and felt helpless, and the only thing that made her feel better was drawing colorful pictures with permanent marker all over her arms and legs.

Fortunately, the aunt had a passion for art, so she offered to have Liza over once a week to draw, paint, and try different types of art. Because Liza really liked spending time with her aunt, she agreed.

They tried watercolor painting and line drawing, but Liza was most excited by oil painting. Liza was intrigued that it could take an oil painting six months to a year to dry. She was fascinated by how she could rework, correct, and scrape off areas of paint and make the picture even better—even after she had painted.

Liza's aunt gradually caught on that Liza was interested in not only this type of art but also what this process symbolized. Growing up took time, and if one day wasn't good, you could try again the next day to make it better. Over time, Liza became more interested in painting on canvas than in coloring herself with markers; she began taking pride in her work.

What You Can Do When You're Concerned

If you find your teenager pursuing a spark that worries you or raises your eyebrows, what can you do?

- *Connect your teenager with adults who share his spark.* For example, if your teenager gets hooked on the electric guitar (and you wish you could move *that noise* to another community), find a good music teacher who has mastered the electric guitar.

- *Figure out what scares you about your teenager's spark.* Sometimes it may be a personality difference, or you have a set of beliefs that are being challenged. For example, a parent who enjoys solitude and reading books may be baffled (and alarmed) by a teenager who likes to spend all her time with friends and coordinate parties. As long as the parties are age appropriate, healthy, and a good place for teenagers, your child may actually be acquiring some important people-organizing skills.

- *Ask your teenager what gets him excited.* Before you dismiss an interest as a passing phase, find out why your teenager enjoys doing a particular activity. Maybe he spends a lot of time copying Manga animation because he is intrigued by the facial expressions of the characters. Filling up sketchbooks is a sign of spark, even if you're not sure what the drawings are all about. (Just ask.)

SPARK STORY
Getting Past an Obsession

Andre couldn't find enough time to rebuild the engine of the used car he had bought. He was obsessed with the car, spending most of his time consumed by this project. If he wasn't working on the car, he was talking about it or researching new ideas on the Internet.

His parents were concerned about Andre, but they were also getting bored. Who wants to talk about one topic all the time? They tried introducing current events during dinnertime, but without success. They tried taking Andre to places he used to love to go (the locomotive part of the museum in their town, for example), but Andre would just sulk—until he thought of something else to talk about changing on his car.

Dauntless, Andre's parents embraced rather than resisted their son's obsession with rebuilding his car's engine. They bought him special books and training materials. They sent him to a special class at the local junior college.

Gradually Andre finished the job and stopped talking about it. He appreciates his parents' support and volunteered to rebuild the family car's engine too, but refrained from talking about it night and day, having regained his spark balance.

If you're concerned that an obsession is going too far, ask for help. Start with someone you know. Sometimes an aunt, uncle, grandparent, or teacher can offer perspective. If that person also is worried, don't be afraid to consult a professional. It often helps to tap the expertise of someone who understands what you and your teenager are going through.

SEE SPARK AS A
LIFELONG JOURNEY

Although the teenage years are critical for following a spark, the process doesn't end when your teenager becomes an adult. In fact, your teenager is just getting started. Pursuing a spark is a lifelong journey. A spark often shows up during childhood, but it deepens during the adult years. For others, a spark shows up later in life, such as when they go to college, when they start their first job, or even later, when the person finds her spark again or for the first time in her thirties, forties, fifties, or older.

What Teens Do Now Matters Later

Having limited contact with adults of various ages makes it difficult for teenagers to understand how they're on a journey where the decisions they make now affect them later on. As adults, we rarely talk about the consequences of actions we took when we were younger or the ways that our present life follows from our past, but young people need to hear about these important connections. This isn't about reminiscing. It's about noticing the mile markers on our spark path.

Think back again to your sparks at age sixteen. Instead of focusing only on the spark itself, now consider other things that influenced and shaped you because of following your spark. For example, maybe you were in Girl Scouts. You earned only a few badges, but every year, you were the top seller of Girl Scout cookies. You're not selling cookies now, but your cookie-selling experience taught you how to talk to people you didn't know, to pitch an idea to someone in a way that got him interested, and to follow through by delivering all the cookies on time. You were passionate about these things, which translated into your current passion for product development. You get excited about something new, know how to pitch the idea to others, and create prototypes that get others excited.

Selling Girl Scout cookies then and doing product development now may seem like very different sparks, and they are—but in name only. How different are they when you begin to break them down? Talking about these connections with your teenager can help her move forward on the spark path—after high school, as a young adult, and as she grows into an older adult.

Stay Involved

This brings us to another important message: as a parent, get involved and stay involved. Even when your teenager leaves home to go to college or to begin work, stay involved. Ask about your child's spark and spark journey. Continue to support and cheer on your child.

Although your teenager is separating from you, he still looks to you for wisdom, guidance, and support. Be engaged in your teenager's life and his spark forever. Let your teenager take the lead in pursuing and deepening his spark, but join him on the journey so that he knows that you believe in him. Even if it feels as if you're showing your support from the sidelines, your teenager notices.

SPARK FACT
The Alarming Decline of Parent Involvement

The percentage of kids who say their parents nurture their spark (by age):

- 91 percent of 10- to 12-year-olds
- 67 percent of 13- to 15-year-olds
- 47 percent of 16- to 18-year-olds

Explore Beyond the Obvious

When Mischa Zimmermann was thirteen, he said his life was "perfect." He made top grades. He was popular, and he was a star player for the soccer team. Then, during a physical exam, the doctor discovered that something wasn't quite right. After a number of tests, the doctors found that Mischa had a malignant tumor in his brain.

Surgery saved his life, but it also radically changed it. Mischa now has double vision and some hearing loss, and he has to use a wheelchair. His voice sounds hoarse and strange because his vocal cords are partially paralyzed.

In the hospital, he discovered how good it felt to help the child in the next bed by letting the boy keep the movie he asked to borrow.

That experience gave Mischa the idea of starting Kids Helping Kids, an organization that helps young people make the transition after a catastrophic illness or injury.

He was able to start something positive out of the difficulty he encountered in life. Wrestling with the spiritual questions also made him stronger. At first, he couldn't figure out why he had gotten this cancer and why his life had changed so radically. But as he struggled with the questions while working on Kids Helping Kids, he gradually achieved some clarity.

"My life is more real now," he said. "I see things I didn't see before. And I've become an advocate. So maybe this all happened for a reason."

A true spark gives life more spirit. "All of the great spiritual traditions want to awaken us to the fact that we co-create the reality in which we live," writes Parker Palmer in *A Hidden Wholeness*. "And all of them ask two questions intended to help keep us awake: What are we sending from within ourselves out into the world, and what impact is it having 'out there'? What is the world sending back at us, and what impact is it having 'in here'?"

Living a life of spark is about living a life of spirit. In the great sacred narratives of the world, this concept of spirit goes by many names, as Palmer reminds us. Buddhists call it "the big self."

Talking about spark, then, is a great way to launch those spiritual conversations you haven't yet gotten around to. These spiritual conversations include topics like these:

- Who are you?

- Why are you here?

- What are your special gifts? Where do they come from?

- How does your life matter?

- How will you make the world a better place?

Rachel Naomi Remen is a clinical professor at the University of California at San Francisco School of Medicine. She is a pioneer in integrating medicine and spiritual practice. She tells a great story she heard from her orthodox rabbi grandfather on her fourth birthday, a story that has stayed with her all her life. You might try telling it to your daughter or son. It comes out of the Jewish mystical tradition of Kabbalah. It goes like this:

"In the beginning, the world was made of light. But by some accident, the light was scattered, and it lodged as countless sparks inside every aspect of creation." So our job as human beings "is to seek this original light in everything and everyone and gather it up, and in so doing, repair or heal the world."

Pursuing a spark pulls people away from thinking only about themselves and what they want to buy. The novel *Babbitt*, by Sinclair Lewis, is a powerful testament to the impoverishment of grounding one's happiness in the shifting sand of status and possessions. In the story, George Babbitt is externally successful, but on the inside, he's miserable. As one reviewer put it, Babbitt seeks happiness in a world that substitutes "stuff" for "soul." This message is as on target now as it was when the book was published in 1922. At the end of the book, Babbitt utters these haunting words: "I've never done a single thing I've wanted to do in my life! I don't know if I've accomplished anything except get along."

Joseph Campbell tells a contemporary version of this tale. He was at dinner in Bronxville, New York, following a day of lectures at Sarah Lawrence College. At the next table sat a mother, a father, and a boy of about twelve.

The dad said to the boy, "Drink your tomato juice."

And the boy said, "I don't want to."

Then the father, raising his voice, yelled, "Drink your tomato juice!"

Then it was Mom's turn. She sternly piped in to the dad, "Don't make him do what he doesn't want to do."

And Dad looked at her and said testily, "He can't go through life doing what he wants to do. He'll be dead. Look at me. I've never done a thing I wanted to do in all my life."

At which point, Campbell reportedly said to himself, "My God, there's Babbitt incarnate!"

Today we have teenagers never doing a single thing they've wanted to in their lives, teenagers doing *only* what they've wanted to do (and not learning the responsibility of being human), and teenagers who fulfill the dream of their spark in a way that takes responsibility for living a life that matters, not only for themselves but also for others.

PART TWO

What Helps
Teens Thrive

CHAPTER ONE

On the Road to a
Hopeful Future
Stories from Across America

One joy scatters a hundred griefs.

—*Chinese proverb*

The thirteen stories in this chapter capture all the dynamics of sparks from teenagers across the country. These are young people who have found their sparks, put them into action, learned from them, and grown as their spark activities stretch them and put them in relationship with spark champions.

These kids know how powerful moms and dads can be, as well as grandparents, teachers, coaches, neighbors, and youth workers.

Together, they stand as a colorful and inspirational portrait of possibility, hope, passion, and exuberance for life. It is a portrait of teenagers America rarely sees.

It is also a portrait of parents who want their children to thrive, to fly with their own specialness. These are parents who do not impose their own definitions of success on their kids. Rather, they let their kids' sparks define what success looks like. They know that a full life is about the journey—the daily-ness of the journey—more than it is about the destination.

Maybe these stories will guide you in becoming that kind of citizen who will always look for the spark, even when surrounding circumstances may suggest nothing but turmoil and heartache. These stories remind all of us of the spark champions who live in our communities. They need our notice, our affirmation, our thanks. These stories are also good for a parent's soul as they refresh and renew our efforts to light our kids' fires and keep them burning.

My hope is that you can read these stories *with* your teenager. Your teen will see herself in these stories. She'll see some of her friends. And if the shared reading of the stories "sparks" conversation, eureka. You'll take it from there.

Where do these stories come from? The best thing about my work at Search Institute is that I get to meet thriving, engaged teenagers in hundreds of cities. For more than a decade, my colleagues and I have been championing a new approach to growing healthy and vibrant young people. This work is rooted in an approach that looks first at young people's strengths and possibilities. The approach names the Developmental Assets that put kids on a hopeful path, and identifies the natural capacity of all towns and cities to generate and nurture these assets if only we can awaken citizens and schools and neighborhoods and families and youth organizations to build sustained, caring relationships with young people. It is across this bridge of adult-youth relationships that so much of what kids need travels. And it is how spark champions emerge for young people. As we often say, relationships are the oxygen of human development.

In preparing this book, we put out the word asking community leaders to identify teenagers whose sparks are visible and contagious. Shelby Andress, master trainer for Search Institute, interviewed each of the nominated teens and captured their stories. These lives will someday be the norm and not the exception.

MARCUS, 14, FRESNO, TEXAS

There are plenty of pressures to get involved in gang violence and drugs in Marcus's community of six thousand outside Houston. But Marcus, who is going into ninth grade, is determined to take a different path.

Marcus says his parents are a big influence. "My parents tell me that if I don't have a direction for my life, then I won't go anywhere, I won't end up where I want to be." His aunt and uncle live next door, and they too encourage Marcus to use his skills to work toward a good career. They talk about engineering or pharmacy or architecture because Marcus is good in math and science. A pastor in his church, who also happens to be an engineer, offers to help Marcus achieve that goal in any way he can. Marcus always knows that when he encounters trouble, he can talk with his parents. "They have inspiring words for me, and they really believe in me."

When Marcus was in fifth grade, a teacher noticed during a track-and-field meet that Marcus was one of the fastest runners in the class, and encouraged him to take up summer track.

"I've been running ever since." That means summers and during the season in school, as well as lots of trips for local and national championships, including meets in San Antonio, Texas, and Orlando, Florida. "I live for track!" Marcus says.

Academics matter for this track team; team members must maintain a C average. "But our coach says we can all do better than C's, and most of us have A's and B's. If one of us is struggling with a class, the rest of us help so they can raise their average."

Teamwork is an important part of running. Marcus tries to be a positive person who can joke, have fun, and encourage his teammates when things are going well and especially when they lose. He figures there's always a next time. And even if they don't win, just the fact that they are running is something to be happy about. So why not enjoy it? He thinks of the skills they are learning—running well, building endurance, and learning smooth transitions in the hand-offs in the four-by-four relay.

But there's more to it than the sport. His overall goal is to keep up his academics and his sport, so that he can apply for a track scholarship for college. That means setting goals for every class and, actually, every day.

His church is an important part of Marcus's life. In that church, whenever a young person gets good grades or graduates or does good things in the community, the pastor makes an announcement about it. "After church, all the adults congratulate you and give you advice and share positive thoughts to encourage you to keep doing well."

How about the drugs and gangs issue? Marcus volunteers with Top Teens of America, which speaks in the community and especially with other young people about having goals, staying out of trouble, and giving service to the community. When he's pressured to get involved in trouble that would push him away from his goals, he says, "Why do you want to get involved in gang violence? You could get shot. Or you could kill somebody and end up in prison. Why would you want to end up there?" About drugs: "Why would you want to do drugs? They can harm your body, hurt your immune system. Or you could die. Why would you want to do that to your body?" He says that when he gives those responses, there's no more pressure on him. People leave him alone.

Marcus is anything but a self-centered athlete. He volunteers in the community, and when Top Teens are with other teens, he keeps his eyes open for kids who need a nudge to follow their interests and find their passion. "I'm highly motivated to understand other kids, to help them find meaning and purpose in their lives." After one of Marcus's speeches about his own life, a young boy came up to him to say he likes to run, too; he followed Marcus's encouragement to join summer track, "and now we're good friends."

"How did I become the person I am today? It is through the love of my parents and my community," Marcus says. "They talk to me;

they care about what I'm doing with my life. They inspire me. They help me stay on track."

KATHRYN, 18, PETAL, MISSISSIPPI

Ask Kathryn what her spark is, and she'll name four: helping others, her family, music, and science. From an early age, Kathryn has grown up in a family and a community that has provided many opportunities for her to discover and pursue her sparks.

"I wouldn't be who I am if it weren't for my family," she says. Her parents, while holding other professional positions, are both performing and teaching musicians. "Our family sings all the time. Someone will burst into song around the house, and pretty soon we'll all be singing." Those spontaneous moments are ones Kathryn says she'll always cherish. Kathryn plays the flute, and she sings in two choirs, one at school and one at church.

Kathryn recently graduated from a high school that places a high value on education. She has been immersed in Advanced Placement (AP) classes throughout high school. In her senior year, she served as student body president and graduated as valedictorian of her Petal High School class.

When you consider Kathryn's high academic achievement together with her interests in science and in helping others, you'll quickly understand why Kathryn plans to pursue a degree in medicine. She's not sure which specialty she'll choose, but she trusts that she will be led, day by day and year by year, to discover her path.

Kathryn's flexibility comes from witnessing and experiencing Hurricane Katrina. Petal, which is one hour north of Biloxi, was hit hard by Katrina. Her area had no electricity, water, or phone service for a week and a half following the storm. Schools were closed for three weeks. Kathryn worked with her family to clear roads of trees, take ice and water to people who had no water, and feed the homeless who slept in her church.

The experience changed Kathryn. "It teaches us not to focus on material things, because we have seen that they can be swept away in a moment." She says she learned to let go of her goals and her plans and to focus on what needed to be done.

Although Kathryn always has had a spark for helping others, Hurricane Katrina cemented her spark and taught her to be even more open. "Look ahead beyond the life you have now," she says when other teenagers ask her how to discover their spark. "Try to see a bigger world." Yet she also knows that who supports you is equally important. "A lot of people strive to succeed," she says. "But some people don't have a spiritual foundation or a strong family supporting them. I know that these supports will help me no matter what changes or challenges I encounter. They won't change. They will always be there."

SPARK QUOTE
Every Teenager Has a Spark

"I believe that every person has a spark in them, something to hold on to. Times will change. Styles will change, but you need something to be grounded in, something [to follow] for the rest of your life."
Kathryn, 18
Petal, Mississippi

ANGELICA, 17, MIDDLETOWN, CONNECTICUT

"When I have a family of my own, I want to raise them exactly as my parents have raised my siblings and me." What is it about the way her parents are raising their children that makes them role models for Angelica, a junior at Middletown High School in Connecticut?

"They always tell us the truth about life. They don't try to paint a pretty picture, but tell us the realities. That makes us trust them more. My dad is really passionate about all of us working hard, getting good grades, and doing well in everything we take on. I wouldn't say he shouts, but he *is* passionate, and we listen to what he says."

The life experiences of Angelica's father and mother have had an impact on their children. In Colombia, their mother was able to complete her college education, but because of economic conditions in that country, their father couldn't finish college. The parents decided, therefore, to come to the United States for the sake of their children, to give them better opportunities.

Angelica greatly respects both of her parents because of the way they live their lives. Because of them, Angelica can follow her sparks. Although Angelica works two jobs, she is crazy about tennis and plays year round, does well academically, and is heavily involved in community and school activities with many service projects. A great joy for her is seeing how happy the children are when she and her classmates put on an Easter egg hunt or a holiday party for them.

Other values from her family take hold, too. "I love fashion, but my mother tells me, 'Who you are is not what you wear. Who you are is what you give back to the world.' My mom keeps me on track with my values," she says.

In her community there's a huge emphasis on Developmental Assets, and she is one of the student leaders on a youth advisory team for the community-wide initiative ACT—Assets Coming Together. This past year, Angelica was given many opportunities in leadership development through this initiative. She has gone all over town talking about assets, why they're important, and what people can do to build assets for and with young people.

Angelica describes herself as a caring person. That's a strength that she sees in herself, as she gives herself fully to other people. "I love people. I love being with them. I love talking with them."

Angelica says her community is reeling because a beloved teacher died suddenly and unexpectedly—a Spanish teacher whom "everyone agrees *was* Middletown High School." That teacher was the most inspiring person in Angelica's life. "She had the most amazing spark that anyone could aspire to—her energy, her altruism, her absolute devotion to making a difference in the lives of people. Every summer she went to Tijuana, Mexico, and lived in a garbage dump where poor people live. She slept in the garbage dump. She ate in the garbage dump, and she taught people—children and adults—to read and write so they could someday get out of that garbage dump. I want to be like her, to be unselfish with my time and put other people first." Angelica's goal of attending college and focusing on becoming a teacher will become one path toward doing the work she loves— on behalf of a larger world.

SPARK QUOTE
Look for Your Spark

"Find out what gives you a sense of purpose. You can't sit back and let it come to you."
Angelica, 17
Middletown, Connecticut

COREY, 16, REESEVILLE, WISCONSIN

Corey is into car racing. He builds racing cars, with help from his dad and other people three times his age whom he has met on the racetrack. His latest car is a junker he bought—"just a piece of metal, a frame"—and rebuilt from the inside out.

Every Saturday night, Corey is on the racetrack, driving at speeds of 90 to 120 miles per hour, trying to stay away from the wall and other cars that might touch his.

"When you're racing, there's no time to think. You hear the other cars that are near you, you hear the noise of your own car, you feel how it shakes. I am bonding with the car. It tells me what I need to do. You really don't think in the car. If you think, you're not driving it."

His love of racing started when he was six years old and watched races when his family lived in Tennessee. His dad, then a mechanic in the military, knew everything about cars and was building his own racing car. When the family moved to Reeseville, Wisconsin, his dad continued his love of racing and started teaching Corey how to build a race car. The young boy even served as part of his dad's pit crew.

This sounds like an exciting life, and right now it is. But that wasn't always so. When Corey was in second grade, some of his teachers, mental health workers, and doctors told his parents that there was no hope for Corey because of his mental health challenges. The family refused to accept that verdict. Still, Corey himself says that until he was about twelve, "I was really a lazy kid. I would just sit around. I didn't do my chores on time. I wasn't responsible. Then one day my dad really confronted me and told me that if I didn't develop some determination, I wasn't going to make it in life. I listened to my dad, and I started to turn my life around." Corey started racing on the tracks when he was fourteen.

"My dad is my inspiration. He's like a legend to me. He is just so cool! He's been in the military, he's a great mechanic, and he races. My mom is terrific, too. She's the owner of my car, my manager, and works to get my sponsorships—people who pay to have their products advertised on my car during races. Money is always an issue. I need the money to buy gas for my car, to pay entry fees for races, to buy my safety equipment, and to pay for all the work I do on the car."

Racing affects every part of Corey's life. He has to be physically fit. He has to keep his grades up so that he can get into North Carolina Tech after high school, because it has a racing school. He works on his car every day, so he doesn't have many friends his own age unless they really like racing, and the only girl friends that really work out are those who love racing and like to help him on his cars. If they don't like racing, they are afraid when they watch him going at high speeds and worry that he'll crash and get hurt. It's not an idle worry. On a recent Saturday night, the front end of Corey's car got torn off. Luckily he wasn't hurt, but there was a lot of rebuilding to do starting Sunday morning.

Most of Corey's friends are older than he—other men at the track, the men on his pit crew. They all want to help him out. In fact, some members of his pit crew have volunteered to work with him because they like the way his teams work together. "You can't have people on your crew that annoy you or each other because they really have to work together and get work done fast."

When Corey shows up at High Expectations, a teen center that serves young people, some of whom have mental health issues, he not only brings his car and tells them about racing but also tells about his own mental health challenges and how he works with them. Once he decided to take charge of his life, Corey started "building character and getting more determined." It all started with a spark, a spark for car racing.

JELEESA, 17, UNION CITY, PENNSYLVANIA

Union City, a few miles inland from Erie, Pennsylvania, has been hit by hard economic times. When walking the streets of Union City, one sees boarded-up storefronts, iridescent orange fencing fallen over on a vacant lot, trash on empty city lots. When people started losing jobs in the area, many moved to Union City to occupy upstairs apartments on Main Street, or anything they could find that was affordable.

Still, there is a devoted group of leaders in the schools and the community who want to make life good for its children and youth. At Search Institute's 2006 Healthy Communities • Healthy Youth conference in Minneapolis, Union City teenagers made a presentation of all that they have done through their Healthy Communities initiative—including cleaning up Main Street and vacant lots, and directly addressing substance abuse and teen pregnancy and sexual activity. That is where we met Jeleesa.

Jeleesa started volunteering with the fire department when she was fifteen. At age sixteen, she qualified for taking an intensive First Responders course. The course was packed with medical information, rescue information, and guidelines for helping people through crises. It was the perfect thing for Jeleesa, whose favorite classes in school are anatomy and physiology.

At seventeen, Jeleesa started getting into the ambulance with the crew of their volunteer fire department—many of whom live on her block in Union City. Jeleesa has comforted spouses who are worried about a loved one who is in crisis. She has seen life in both sad and wonderful moments.

"I've seen a person die, and that was really sad. Another time a person was unconscious when we got there, and actually died, but our team was able to bring him back to life. That was a wonderful thing to see." Jeleesa explains, when asked what motivates her to walk into crisis situations, "If you didn't want to help people when they're hurting, you wouldn't be willing to go on these calls."

This interest in helping people who are hurting didn't just pop up at age fifteen. Since she was a little girl, Jeleesa has felt deeply for her friends who were physically hurt or feeling bad about something. She always wanted to be there for them, to comfort them, to help in any way she could. "You have to be there for them, even if you're scared."

Jeleesa's interest in caring for people also extends to concern for her peers. She's part of a peer education team of youth from her school who speak with students about Search Institute's 40 Developmental Assets, relating those assets to concerns about substance abuse and teen pregnancy. "Our numbers of teen pregnancies skyrocketed this year, so it was a really big concern." The coordinator of that project is aware that many students will listen to their peers, so she arranges opportunities for presentations in the area.

Jeleesa lives with her grandparents, and she credits them for always being there for her. "They're always pushing me to do well in school and tell me that they will help me in every way they can." She sings the praises of her mother, as well, who went through difficult struggles as a young woman and now has turned her life around. Although they don't live together, Jeleesa talks to her mother on the phone twice a day. Jeleesa says her mother tells her, "You can do it. You can hang in there and carry out your dreams."

Pursuing her passion means that Jeleesa has had to give up some things that have been hard to give up. In her junior year, she couldn't be on the cheerleading squad because she chose to work to pay for her car insurance and her cell phone. Her life is really busy, between school assignments, working to pay bills, and volunteering. She is intent on getting good grades so that she can qualify for scholarships to a university in her area.

Her community is something she cares about greatly. "Our community has gone through a lot. Industries left town; businesses closed down. Our Healthy Communities leader is really committed to bringing everyone together again, making us whole as a community."

In fact, it's individuals in the community who help support Jeleesa's spark. "I have lots of people in my life who help me," she says.

DEMETRIO, 19, QUEEN ANNE'S COUNTY, MARYLAND

Ask Demetrio where he found his spark, and he'll point to his community, Queen Anne's County. It's the largest county on the eastern shore of Maryland, comprising about twenty different little towns.

"We have all different ethnic backgrounds, and everyone you meet was here from the beginning," he says "Everywhere I go, someone always knows me and is willing to give a helping hand. My aunt was my kindergarten teacher, and she taught all the grandchildren in our whole extended family, as well as all the great-grandchildren. Most of my teachers taught my mother and my grandmother. They always looked out for me. Always there was an encouraging word, someone reinforcing me."

Demetrio laughs when he says, "I was raised by my mother, my grandparents, *and* my great-grandparents. No, we didn't live in the same house. In fact, I had a bedroom in three different houses all the time I was growing up. It was just a matter of 'well, whose house will I sleep at tonight?'" He was welcomed everywhere, as were all his cousins. No matter which house he was in, he always heard the same message from his family: do what you have to do; go to school; pray to the Lord every day.

From the time he was five years old, Demetrio knew he wanted to be a teacher, and he told everyone he met. "In my family, everyone becomes either a teacher or a pastor," he says. Whenever his mother or grandmother went into a store, they bought him something pertaining to education—a blackboard, a book, posters, artwork. "Believe it or not, my bedroom was set up like a classroom!" His library has more than two thousand books in it, most of them about education. "I read those books at night, and before I go to sleep I pray to the Lord to make me as good a person as the wonderful teachers who wrote those books."

Reading hundreds of books has presented a huge challenge for Demetrio. He struggled with a reading disability all through elementary school, requiring special education classes. Middle school teachers turned that around. "The middle name of one of my teachers was Pushed! English was her passion. She really pushed me. She made me read everything out loud, she sent home great big assignments, and she taught me lots of strategies for reading well. I still use those strategies today." Another teacher told him she had had the same problem at the same age, and talked to him about how she had worked through it.

In tenth grade, Demetrio's English teacher didn't realize he'd had reading problems, and she told him, "I'm going to help you get ready for college." Soon he was reading at a twelfth-grade level. He stayed on the honor roll throughout his high school career.

Opportunity jumped in when Demetrio was fifteen, when his school district invited him to teach character education each week in elementary school classrooms. In his work with elementary school children, Demetrio considers one of his most important strengths to be empowerment. He wants to empower children to move beyond their fears. He also uses his exuberant creativity in that work.

"People look at me kind of weird sometimes. I'll wear weird clothes, bright clothes, weird shoes, funky hair."

It's his way of telling other people that they, too, can use their creativity to announce, "I am special, I am unique." When a six-year-old in one of his character education classes had cancer and lost her hair because of chemotherapy, Demetrio went out and bought all pink clothes—her favorite color—and wore them to school, then shaved his head to show solidarity.

The child's hair wasn't growing back, so Demetrio kept shaving his head. He said to the child, "If you rub my hair very gently, I'm sure that will help the hair grow back in." This helped the child think about other things than her cancer and her chemotherapy. Demetrio told the child's mother not to tell her child that he was shaving his head and waiting until the girl's hair started growing. When the child's hair grew back in, Demetrio let his hair grow back in as well, and pointed out how she had helped his hair grow back. The girl is now eight and is doing well.

Demetrio's great-grandfather was his inspiration for creativity and his determination to overcome his obstacles and achieve his goals. "My great-grandfather was one of the most creative men you could ever find on this planet. He had his own company. He fixed lawnmowers and painted them with fun and colorful designs. He would tell all the grandchildren and great-grandchildren, 'Please, use your creativity!'" The elderly man's passion for church helped "me understand that I can have passion, determination, and do it!" Although his grandfather was untrained in music, he formed a singing group of men from all over the county. Called the New Tones, they sang gospel and spirituals. One of their songs became a theme of Demetrio's life: "Always Give 101 Percent."

SPARK QUOTE
Keep Trying Until You Find Your Spark

"Everyone has a gift, a talent. If it doesn't work the first time, pick out something else and run with it."
Demetrio, 19
Queen Anne's County, Maryland

KALIA, 17, MINNEAPOLIS, MINNESOTA

Kalia was born in California, the daughter of Hmong immigrants from Laos. She now lives in Minneapolis and is on her way to college, with the dream of majoring in criminal justice.

"When I was in elementary school and middle school, I was really shy. I mostly stayed to myself and didn't talk much with other people. Then during my sophomore year, a police officer visited our school and talked to a class. She invited us to join PAL [Police Athletic League], and I thought, 'Here's my chance!'"

For the past three years, Kalia has been going to PAL every Monday night. She and the other involved teens are given simulations in police activities, such as conducting searches, controlling traffic, or dealing with domestic conflicts. They work as teams of four students, and the police officers are judges who rate them on their team's accuracy.

"Being in PAL has helped me in school. I've been captain of our school basketball team, and I'm also strong in softball. Through PAL, I've learned teamwork and leadership. I've been treasurer, secretary, and president of the Student Senate, which is a service organization in the community and in the school. Hmong club and drama club—I've been active in those groups, too. I'm a very positive person, and I like to encourage people, joke around, and help people relax and just do their best, even if we don't win (in sports or in police work competitions). I always figure there's another time when we might do better, and after all, we're a team, so for now, just enjoy it."

Kalia says her family is supportive of her pursuing her passion for being a police officer. She says her father grew up in Laos without a father, and he didn't have opportunities to do what he wanted. Still, her father discovered a passion for mechanics. He learns everything he can about cars, and he's a terrific mechanic. "He cheers me on, and tells me I can do it. Even though some members of my family worry about the danger in police work, they believe in me, and they don't hassle me about my choice."

Kalia's idol is a police officer, a woman who has stuck with her all the way. "What does she do that inspires me? For one thing, she will do anything, everything, to help other people. The day I had to do my fitness tests—and they are really grueling tests—she was with me every minute. On the tests that I knew I'd have a hard time with, she'd look me straight in the eye, and she'd keep looking at me, and she'd say, 'Come on, you can do it, Kalia. You can make this one.' And I'd keep on, reaching the goal and even doing better than the goal on some of the exercises."

Because Kalia has experienced the power of people taking an interest in her, she has decided to help those younger than she. She works as a volunteer with children in her church. She helps them with crafts, games, and songs every Saturday. "I love being with those children, and they know that. I keep thinking that maybe I can be a role model for them, and they will want to pursue a positive goal in their lives, too. And when they're older and I see them on the streets, they will feel comfortable with me, and if they need help, I can be there for them."

Next year, Kalia plans to attend a university in her community that has a special commitment to Hmong people. "They gave me a good scholarship, and they have a major in law enforcement. I can't think of anything that will get in the way of my goal, because I am so sure of what I want to do. I just have to keep working hard to achieve it. Besides that, I have so much support from my family, my police officer mentor, and the pastors and a police officer in my church.

"I am determined to be a police officer, especially now that so many Hmong people are moving into Minneapolis. There will be so many children and young people that I can help."

MICHAEL, 16, SEYMOUR, CONNECTICUT

"Since I was a little kid, I've always liked to look at the sky. I like to notice different cloud formations. It makes me really aware of my environment, even wary, because you can see, for example, if there's going to be a storm, and you can warn people."

Michael watches the Weather Channel regularly. Studying the environment, he is acutely aware of global warming and is immersed in atmosphere science, learning about greenhouse gases and what they are doing to our planet.

Becoming a meteorologist has been a lifelong passion for Michael. He wants to help determine the quality of life for future generations. His interest in math and science has led him to take honors and AP courses as one way to ensure that he can get into a good college to pursue meteorology. "I want to get the best grades I can possibly get."

Still, when asked what his spark is, what gives him joy and energy and purpose in life, he quickly responds, "My family is definitely my spark! The most important thing in life is to have a good relationship with your family. You will grow up happy and healthy. You need your parents in order to be successful because they teach you morals and right behavior. My parents are helping me along the way. They are there supporting me whenever I have a new idea. I know they will always be there for me." His friends are important to Michael, too. "They really do help you. Their lives reflect on your life."

Michael is close not only to his parents but also to his grandmother. "My grandma is my hero. She is really strong. She's always there for you, to help you through things. She has a great personality, and everyone can get along with her."

Michael sees his grandmother every week, and when he was younger, they always spent Fridays together, while his parents were at work. They'd go to a mall or see a movie or do things together that they both could enjoy, and they'd "talk about everything." He admires her because when she moved from New York City (population 8.2 million) to the rural town of Seymour, Connecticut (population now about fifteen thousand), she had to make a lot of changes in her life. Her life has helped Michael learn that the person you become depends a lot on where you live at various points in your life and how you adapt to changes, no matter what age you are.

It's a two-way street between Michael and his grandmother. He helps her around the house, and he has taught her how to use the computer. She now uses Web pages to look up things that interest her, such as new recipes. The two of them talk through e-mails, and she now likes to send e-mails to family members and friends.

Michael's life extends beyond himself and his family. Every week, he works as a volunteer in the offices of the School for Ethical Education (SEE), helping on the computer, preparing spreadsheets for the data that SEE collects on its service learning and character education projects. He admires the work of SEE, which sponsors events that help children grow up to have better lives. Especially satisfying was helping generate ideas for a sizeable grant awarded to SEE for its work with Michael's high school.

Even with his family, academic strengths, and active volunteerism, Michael acknowledges that there are barriers to overcome.
"In everything you deal with in life, there always are obstacles. You
have to go around them. For me, there really haven't been big barriers, but I know that the cost of college will be pretty overwhelming. Still, that won't get in the way." Michael figures that if obstacles
do come up, such as learning in college that he really isn't as interested in meteorology as he's always thought he was, then there will
be other things he can do. He will explore any opportunities that
he sees open to him. "You can always find out what works for you,
what interests you, and go for that."

"I believe there is pretty much a spark in everybody's life. You
need to have something to look forward to in life, something that
makes you feel better. You have to pursue your dreams in life. Maybe
I sound more like an adult than a teenager when I say that, but
that's what I believe."

SPARK QUOTE
Follow Your Unique Path

"Follow your own ideas instead of falling to peer pressure. Develop what
you believe you should do, not what some kid you know says you should
do. Act on the qualities that make you a unique person."

Michael, 16

Seymour, Connecticut

CASSIE, 18, GRANT CITY, MISSOURI

For Cassie, growing up in Grant City, Missouri, a community of
fewer than a thousand people and a high school of two hundred students, has given her the greatest life she could imagine.

Do you need to be in a big school in order to find your spark and
succeed? Not when a guidance counselor offers a class for gifted

and talented students, or where teachers arrive early and leave late in order to help students do well, or another teacher doubles up a teaching load and offers AP courses.

And what about things to do? Cassie has participated in sports, drama, choir, glee club, marching band, concert band, National Honor Society, Academic Bowl, FCCLA (Family, Career, and Community Leaders of America), FBLA (Future Business Leaders of America), and in such service projects as caroling at nursing homes, volunteering at a thrift store, and being a Memorial Day volunteer.

How can a place with limited financial resources offer its young people so many opportunities?

"This town lives for its young people," Cassie says. "Every time the school wants to do something, we have to have a fundraising campaign. We always go to the same people. When students volunteered to resurface a basketball court downtown or to plant trees in front of the new school library, those people supported us all the way." And when it comes to sports events or anything else at the school, the whole town turns out.

Although there can be disadvantages in a small town where everyone knows everyone else, Cassie finds that intimacy a plus. Her grandpa, who died several years ago, was a skilled woodworker who did beautiful work for everybody in town. He also played the piano for local shows all around the area. As a young child, Cassie watched how interested he was in people, how he could make them laugh, how much people loved being around him, the way they respected him.

She remembers her grandfather every day, and his memory guides her when she visits a nursing home in town or helps a "sub" in math class by working individually with students who are struggling with their math that day.

Her parents and siblings (a sister and two brothers) all stick together through thick and thin. Cassie respects all of them because they are successful in the kinds of people they are—helping whoever needs help, for example, which can include dropping by her grandma's house to help out, or driving to town when a friend needs a ride. Their values don't focus on the amount of money people make, but on the goals they set, their hard work. That's a huge family value: hard work, giving up personal "down" time in order to achieve a goal or help others.

There have been hard times. Recently Cassie's mother had cancer, and Cassie says that the community carried them through it every step of the way. Every day at school, and especially when teachers noticed that Cassie "might have been behaving a little differently," they would ask if she was okay and want to know how her mom was doing. Cassie herself focused on school and sports, and especially wanted to make sure that her little brother was doing okay during their mother's illness. (Her mother is doing well now.)

Despite the hardships, Cassie doesn't worry about the future. Most important to her is "making sure I have the people who are important to me, to help me through everything."

When asked how she became the person she is today, Cassie's response is clear and quick: "My family! They are 100 percent supportive of whatever I do. I watch how happy members of my family are. They all have been so successful at whatever they are happy doing. My parents love each other. They are happy with their life. They love their kids.

"My parents always say, 'Go ahead, try it, see if you like it.' They didn't tell me that I could be in only one sport or one activity. They encourage all of us to 'do whatever you want to do.'"

MAX, 16, NEW GROVE, PENNSYLVANIA

If Max is interested in anything—*anything*—he does research on it. That curiosity extends from computers to Web site businesses, from sports to nature, from music to writing. "If I find inspiration and motivation, then I just do it."

Max says he definitely has more than one spark. "A lot of things in life inspire. A lot! I guess my sparks would fall into four categories:

family and friends, learning and education, personal interests like drums and computers, and sports and my own physical exercise program."

Max discovered his sparks through his sophomore language arts teacher at the Media, Pennsylvania, high school. "For most of my life, I thought I was just an ordinary person without a very interesting life. But my teacher pointed out to me that I really do have curiosity and a lot of motivation to learn just about anything." What is that teacher like? What does he say or do that has turned around Max's view of himself? "He's always giving us great lessons on life, and he made me notice these things in my life."

Max credits great teachers for showing him how he could work hard and have fun at the same time. "That's very important, having fun learning, because if you aren't having fun, then you're not going to learn much."

Max's curiosity and passion for learning started with his parents, who encouraged him to take on anything that interested him. "I'm very fortunate to have the parents I have. They are very easy for me to talk with about school, about friends, about any issues that come up."

His parents show support for Max's learning in practical ways as well. Max usually studies downstairs in the house, and his parents will come down and say, "Max, are you getting along all right with your homework? Do you need help with anything?" Max says he doesn't like to ask for help, so they make it easy for him by taking the initiative. He thinks that a lot of kids think they should be able to do their homework all on their own but are often grateful when parents offer to help.

Max's parents model the spark-filled life. His dad is a microbiologist who is serious about his work. His mother, a nurse practitioner, works intensely with people all day and puts her entire self into her job. Max says he has been known to take off his mother's glasses when she falls asleep at eight o'clock at night. "I don't believe either of them could do what they do without a spark."

What's Max's latest learning project? Computers and Web design. In his community, the Healthy Community initiative has a great Web site. Max volunteers once a week to update the Web site, and his mentor is a man at Picture Syndicate in downtown Media.

Now Max wants to start a Web site business with a school friend, but they don't know about the business side of Web sites, so they're going to do research on how to get clients, how to serve them, and how to handle the finances. Their hope is to start their business during their junior year in high school.

Max knows that improving his time management skills is key for developing any spark. "When new sparks appear, it's important for me to practice good time management, especially with my interest in drums and computers. I have to keep up with my interests and make sure I do what I've said I'll do. Even if that means spending only fifteen minutes a day on it, I'll do it."

Two words come up again and again in Max's life: motivation and inspiration. "It's very important that I discovered these within myself. I know my family and friends have motivated me, but it's my personal willingness, my personal will, that makes the difference. I want to meet new people, learn new things, and keep in shape. If I find that I really don't like something, I'll stop. It's up to me."

LAUREN, 18, ELLICOTT CITY, MARYLAND

"Sometimes I feel like the most fortunate person on the face of this planet. My family is strong and intact, I have great parents, and I live in a very international, multicultural family that gets along well. Yes, we are a family with many privileges, but my parents emphasize doing work that contributes to the world in a significant way. And they live their own lives that way as well."

Lauren feels deeply about the privilege of knowing her extended family. Her father was raised Jewish; her mother, an Italian Catholic, converted to Judaism; one of her mother's sisters married a Hindu from India; another, a man from Puerto Rico; another, a French Canadian.

That privilege goes deeper than enjoying one another across cultural and religious traditions, however. During her growing up years, Lauren and her mother took long walks together, and "my mother always talked with me, adult to adult, telling me about her relationships and her thoughts about life, so I got to know her really well, the struggles and the joys." Neither of her parents ever treated her like a baby or intervened when she bumped into an obstacle. They'd encourage her to work things out for herself.

She remembers especially well how she felt at the age of ten when her family moved from Tennessee to Maryland. She was a new kid trying to fit in. It was a difficult time, as she was "just a floater." During that period in her life, she wrote in a journal, and "I developed a proclivity for observing people, understanding what makes them behave as they do."

That independent spirit served her school well when she became president of Junior Statesmen of America (JSA) during the year of a presidential election. Students in JSA became active politically, had debates and discussion groups, and kept informed. "As president, I had to know what we were talking about. I had to have a depth of knowledge."

Lauren's passion for international relations focuses on humanitarian aid. She has traveled extensively with her family and has seen some of the worst of poverty and misery in the world. It's that misery that she wants to address. Her biggest challenges, she will tell you, are that she has to learn that she can't change the world quickly or alleviate people's suffering the way she wants to, and that she hasn't experienced firsthand what it's like to have so little of life's bounty.

Leadership opportunities have broadened her spark for international affairs, especially her work with the Horizon Foundation, a community foundation that extends multiple kinds of leadership and assistance in Howard County, Maryland. Serving on the executive board as a youth representative, and also on the Connections youth board, Lauren has learned about the nonprofit world and the many needs that social sector organizations try to meet. The youth board develops a budget and funding priorities, receives requests for funding, and makes hard decisions about which projects to fund for youth development in the county.

Social justice is much more than a lofty ideal for Lauren; it's very hands-on. One of the most satisfying experiences of her life was leading a three-day regional conference of the North American Federation of Temple Youth in the mid-Atlantic region. They studied social justice issues. They went out into the community, partnering with many justice-oriented organizations. Their final challenge was to prepare lobbying positions and actually do lobbying with invited local political leaders.

"The way it all came together, after all those months of planning, was incredible!" It definitely was a high point in her life and for everyone who came together around their common cause and vision.

Music was something Lauren at one time dropped "cold turkey" because she thought she didn't have time for it. But then some friends encouraged her to try out for a madrigal singing group. From there, Lauren went on to have roles in musicals and plays. Her favorite was being the mother of Helen Keller in *The Miracle Worker*. "When you act, you get inside people's lives"; this was what she liked most about acting.

Where did her spark come from? The influences extend beyond family. Lauren points to teachers, adult leaders of the clubs she's in, and her neighbors.

"When I take my little brother to the bus stop (he's seven), all the elementary moms, and a couple of dads, are there with their kids, standing around talking. They're all interested in me, what I'm doing, how things are going. A next-door neighbor spent hours and hours helping us through the application process for college."

SPARK QUOTE
Think Bigger

"Do work that contributes to the world in a significant way."
Lauren, 18
Ellicott City, Maryland

MILES, 18, MIDDLETON, CONNECTICUT

"My spark would definitely be music," says Miles, who is heading for Berklee College of Music in Boston, where he hopes to major in music performance. "Music opens up a new world for me, whether it's studying music theory or listening to music. I need it in my life."

Miles grew up in a musical family. His father is a musician, and his mother is an artist who also sings. Their house, he says, is stuffed with records, instruments, and books. "I've been around music all my life," he says.

In fact, a favorite family story is about Miles at the age of twelve months, picking up a drumstick and tapping on a drum in perfect rhythm. At the age of nine, when his family was visiting a cousin, Miles discovered a full drum set in the basement. He spent the entire vacation in the basement, so the next year, his parents bought him his own drum set and started him with drum lessons.

Miles is so passionate about music that he helps younger kids make music. This past summer, Miles led a group of kids in grades 4 through 12 to make their own hip-hop CD. Students wrote the lyrics and the music. They designed the CD cover, and they were in charge of distributing it.

Yet Miles is concerned about people the kids idolize. Many point out to Miles that the rap music star Fifty Cent became rich and didn't even go to high school. Miles doesn't like that message. He thinks school is important—and so is setting a good example. He dislikes music that degrades women and other people, and he resents that the music industry promotes those kinds of lyrics. "I admire people who have songs you can sing," he says, "who make really good music, really deep music, and can really express themselves."

For Miles, music is it. "I feel like music is always there for me," he says. "At night when I go to bed, I'm listening to music. When I wake up, I listen to music again." If he's not listening to music, then he's playing it—every day, three to four hours a day, alone or with friends. It doesn't matter, as long as it's music.

PHIL, 18, MINNEAPOLIS, MINNESOTA

During his senior year, Phil wasn't sure he would walk across the stage at graduation with the rest of his class. He found it difficult to latch on to his course work when he wanted so much to be a part of things in the real world.

"I felt sorry for my mother. Practically her full-time job was volunteering in schools and instilling the value of education, and now she was watching her son who acted as though education wasn't of any value." Yet he managed to pull up his grades by the end of his senior year and earn his diploma.

About three years before graduating, Phil found himself struggling with depression. A friend came into his life during that difficult time. She was a teenager, but to Phil she was a wise psychologist who helped him a lot. Her dad had an advanced degree in theology and loved to talk about matters of faith.

"I started searching for the relationship between my politics, the secular world, my own faith, and a call to service. I discovered that I like theology for its cerebral side." He credits these deep conversations with several people for bringing him out of his depression and setting him on a path to follow his spark.

Part of that path involved remembering what got him excited when he was younger. Phil remembered watching the Democratic National Convention on TV as an eight-year-old and sensing that he needed to make a difference in the world: to bring justice and to help those in need.

The challenge, however, was that Phil didn't find it easy to follow the conventional paths that others took. His high school course work was difficult because he liked focusing on one thing at a time, not changing subjects every hour. Once his depression lifted, he got excited about music theory, composition, and performing in a musical duo with a high school friend. Together they recorded a CD of the music they composed together. He liked following his own spark, rather than getting involved in organized high school activities.

After high school, Phil was joking around with a friend and asked, "Why don't we just go to Africa?" That was another part of Phil's spark—thinking out of the box, thinking of the impossible. He was surprised when his friend said yes. She had been to Africa when she was nine years old. Her family had contacts with many organizations in Uganda. If he really wanted to go, she would go with him.

The two families met, and the girl's family connected Phil and the girl with an organization in Uganda. They set out to do six months of service in that country.

Living in Uganda changed Phil's view of education. He learned that "no matter what we might prefer, we are growing up in a system of education and we have to complete certain tasks." In retrospect, he wishes he'd taken high school more seriously, but he realized he was still learning. Learning didn't stop after high school graduation.

Phil says he took away more from Africa than he gave. He was surprised by how much you could learn from another culture. "One big thing is time management. It doesn't exist in Africa. Here in the United States, we are regimented down into two-minute increments. In Africa, there's a lot of space to live in the moment, like seeing the wind moving through the trees. I was incredibly moved by that, those simple things we could notice and take into ourselves. It's much harder here."

Materialism in his own country shook him, too, when he came back. "It really hurt a lot, walking into a store and seeing someone buying a lava lamp. I'd think, in Uganda that much money could pay tuition for three kids to go to school for a whole year. Why would anyone want to pay all that money for a lava lamp?"

For Phil, the trip to Uganda helped him see the relationship between faith, justice, politics, and his own life work. He realized that even though he had struggled through high school, he has a great intellectual curiosity about many things and enjoys asking deep philosophical questions. He also knows that his questions lead him to action.

Most recently, Phil has been helping a friend who has been in and out of rehab a few times but is now dedicated to sobriety. "He likes to cook, so I've been getting him charged up about cooking, and now he's thinking seriously of going to culinary school." Phil now sees that his past of barely graduating from high school can be an inspiration to others. "I can say, 'Okay, I was a screw-up in high school, but I'm doing okay now . . . and you can too.'"

For Phil, his challenge and opportunity are about having a spark that isn't specific and concrete. How does one integrate a passion for justice, philosophy, and politics? Phil doesn't have the answer yet, but he's enjoying following those sparks and seeing where they lead. He says life doesn't get much better than that.

CHAPTER TWO

Thriving Youth, Thriving Nation

thrive v **1:** *to prosper* **2:** *to grow or develop vigorously*
3: *to flourish*

Thrive is an active verb, a process. A spark is the central metaphor I use to understand the human process of thriving. A spark is an interest, talent, or skill that animates one's life, giving it energy and focus. When we express a spark, we feel alive. We feel useful. Life has a purpose.

Most teenagers get the concept of spark in the blink of an eye. They know if they've got it. They can easily see it when it's there.

As we saw earlier, the most common category of sparks for teenagers is the creative arts. Music, art, dance, and writing are mentioned twice as often as sports. Yet you'd never know it by how local communities make their investments. We seem to think that drawing, painting, sculpting, playing an instrument, composing music, writing lyrics, sketching, singing, dancing, acting, writing poetry, and creating stories are merely nice things to do. We think engagement in this soft and artsy stuff can round out a person and perhaps even deflect young people from negative peer pressure or risk-promoting situations.

SPARK QUOTE
Have Courage

"It takes courage to grow up and turn out to be who you really are."
e. e. cummings

But these perceptions are never forceful enough to move the creative arts to center stage. Band, orchestra, theater, and dance always yield when money is needed for "real" academic investment. It's never the other way around. Even worse is the pressure to invest in football and other big-time sports at the expense of the creative arts.

One of the central tenets of child development is the primacy of play. I recently heard several public school teachers lament that there's not time for play anymore in kindergarten and in first through third grade. Instead, school officials want more time for arithmetic drills because early preparation predicts higher test scores in fourth grade.

Our teenagers are feeling the negative effects of this go-go-go and keep-learning-learning-learning mentality. Many of them are finding themselves living the rat-race lives of their parents, working all the time and finding it impossible to keep up.

Yet spark changes all that. A spark is not about getting the highest test scores, even though a teenager who has a spark and at least three spark champions tends to get higher grades in school. A spark is about living a life that matters, one that your teenager really wants to live.

SPARK QUOTE

Spark: What We're Really Looking For

"People say that what we're all seeking is meaning in life. I don't think that's what we're really seeking. I think what we're seeking is an experience of being alive, so that our life experiences on the purely physical plane will have resonance within our own innermost being and reality, so that we actually feel the rapture of being alive."
Joseph Campbell

THE KEY SPARK LESSONS

Seven key lessons have been woven throughout this book. Each is supported by our new research on sparks and spark champions and the implications for the well-being of our young. The seven lessons are

1. Kids understand the idea of sparks and want them.
2. A majority of young people have a spark and can describe it.
3. Expand your view of what sparks can be.
4. Parents should be spark team captains.
5. Sparks need other spark champions in addition to parents.
6. Great things happen when kids pursue their sparks.
7. Most teens don't have enough spark champions in their lives.

There's an eighth lesson. I have been dancing around it in previous chapters. Now is a good time to name it: sparks and generosity go hand in hand.

Sparks and Generosity

Some might think that a focus on one's own passion and joy is a path to hedonism, to self-centeredness. Much to the contrary:

teenagers with sparks and spark champions are *more* likely to volunteer in their communities. Profiles of youth with spark across America are chock-full of dedication to service, generosity, and social justice. It's as though the process of being grounded in one's true essence opens a life to the world. This is, for me, the most treasured aspect of a life of following one's spark.

SPARK QUOTE
Keep Your Spark Lit and Burning Bright

"Life is no brief candle for me. It is a sort of splendid torch which I have got hold of for the moment, and I want to make it burn as brightly as possible before handing it on to future generations."
George Bernard Shaw

A life of sparks speaks loudly and positively to the issues of generosity of spirit, of commitment, passion, and purpose. And a life of sparks also speaks to the issues of obligation and responsibility. These are big issues of moral development. How do I make the world a better place? How do I lead a life that matters for others?

Young people on the path of following their sparks are more likely to reach out and more likely to be stewards of the environment. As a life finds its center, as a life finds its anchor, it does not become selfish. On the contrary, it becomes generous.

This connection between sparks and generosity has two variants. Sometimes it is about using one's spark to enlighten the journey of another. For example, Gregg Petersmeyer has dedicated his life to making volunteerism a central principle of our national life. He's been an advocate as a member of the White House staff, as a nonprofit executive, and as a policymaker. He gave me a great idea, which I now pass on to you.

If your child has an identifiable spark, ask this question: "Now that you know your spark, how can you use it to make life better for others?"

Or, as Gregg suggests, you might actually provide an avenue for sharing. Let's say the spark is chess. Then here's the question: "Would you be willing to teach it to younger children in a local grade school or in an after-school program?" Then be prepared to ask around and find the opportunity. It will be one of the most precious gifts you ever give your child.

Generosity, Sacrifice, and Service

Pilar Gonzales learned about generosity by being on the receiving end of it as a child and teenager. She grew up in a migrant farm-working family. Her dad picked cherries in Michigan, and she often helped him as a child. When Pilar turned nineteen, she struggled to find a job and ended up homeless for six months, begging for money and sleeping under trees.

When Pilar finally found a job, she also discovered her spark. She decided to give away a portion of what she earned. Last year, she earned $16,000. She gave away $8,000.

Yes, she has learned to become content with fewer material possessions. Pilar lives in a one-bedroom apartment decorated with secondhand furniture. She doesn't own many clothes, but she says it's worth it—in order to pursue her spark. In winter, she hands out gloves and hats, lined with five-dollar bills. In summer, she distributes water bottles to the migrant workers and day laborers.

As it did for Pilar, sometimes the engagement in service unleashes the spark. That is, serving is itself the spark. It is hard to imagine anything better for a nation than to awaken this passion, this spark, in young lives.

SPARK STORY

Marion Wright Edelman

Founder and President of the Children's Defense Fund

Adults in Marion Wright Edelman's early years both crystallized her spark and pushed her to find outlets for it. "I and my brothers and sister might have lost hope—as so many young people today have lost hope—except for the stable, caring, attentive adults in our family, school, congregation, civic and political life who struggled with and for us against the obstacles we faced and provided us positive alternatives and the sense of possibility we needed."

Edelman's lifelong spark has been as an activist committed to "changing the world" for children. She knew it at an early age. And she was embedded in a series of relationships that modeled and nurtured this devotion to change.

THE TOP TEN SPARK LIST

Toward that end, I offer a summary of ten guidelines for parents that have been sprinkled throughout this book. Consider this your top ten spark list:

1. Every teenager has one or more sparks. Sometimes the spark is hidden or dormant, but it is there.

2. Sparks can change. A spark at age sixteen may look different from a spark at twelve.

3. Sparks are not learned. They originate from inside a person and are discovered and nourished through experience.

4. The hallmark of spark is not happiness or pleasure, but passion.

5. Every parent has the capacity to be a spark champion.

6. The better you model a life with sparks, the more likely it is that your child will develop a life with spark at the center.

7. A person's spark is her unique song. Remember to hum it back to your teenager on days when she doesn't remember it.

8. Your teen needs not only you as a spark champion but other adults as well.

9. Trust the spark.

10. Ask the question, "Now that you know your spark, how can you use it to make life better for others?"

SPARK TIP
Advice from Tom Keiffer

Tom Keiffer is a dedicated parent, inquisitive soul, and successful entrepreneur, and in that order. He has asked many parents, "What's the one piece of advice you have about how to be a great parent?" And the two answers Tom has hung onto for years are

- Find your child's passion and do everything you can to support it.

- Always try to find a way to say yes.

It would be worth writing these two maxims down and putting them in your day planner, on your computer, or on the mirror in your bathroom. They are that useful and important.

THRIVING WITH SPARKS

Spark is not an end point. It's a process. As a gardener, I think about plants that thrive, or fail to, in the shade that bathes my yard in Minnesota. Some plants flourish; some wither. It is a matter of how the essence of a plant becomes embedded in the right mixtures of soil and air and temperature and nutrients.

My pediatric friends and colleagues remind me that nearly all hospitals, in the birthing room, use a measurement called the Apgar score. It assesses a newborn's color, heart rate, response to stimulation of the sole of the foot, muscle tone, and respiration. A high score means that the newborn in thriving. What's interesting to me about this is that it is the only measure of thriving I know of, and it is administered in the first hour of life. Why do we not assess thriving at age ten or fifteen or thirty-five?

As a parent, I always wonder if my adult kids are thriving. I care much less about their achievements and much more about the daily quality of their lives. Are they doing what they are called to do? And now as a grandparent, I use the idea of thriving to understand my grandson's development. His name is Ryder. As he turned four, I overheard this conversation:

Ryder: "Ask me why I am skipping."

Moma (his grandmother): "Okay, Ryder, why are you skipping?"

Ryder: "Because I'm so happy to be in the world."

I take those words as evidence that Ryder is on a path to a hopeful future. Right now, he is thriving. It is early, but what a great start.

How many of us can say, "I am skipping because I'm so happy to be in the world"? If we can't, it is time to reassess.

As a social scientist, I have been thinking and writing a lot about the meaning of thriving. It is this work that led me to the idea of spark as the animating force that helps us grow vigorously.

The dynamic model of thriving has a number of features. To be precise, there are twenty-four components of a thriving life, which appear in the checklist that follows. You will recognize most of them from this book. You can put checks in the boxes next to the elements that you think your child already has. This checklist can serve as a road map to guide you in advancing your child's thriving.

In this model of thriving, I put as much emphasis on the "soil" (the people and places to which your child is connected) as I do on the "seed" (your child). In so doing, I follow one of the maxims of human developmental psychology: a person's development is about the dynamic interplay between that person and the environments that nourish (or block) his or her development. Hence, I think of thriving as *the dynamic interplay of a young person animated and energized by discovering his or her specialness, and the developmental contexts (people, places) that know, affirm, celebrate, encourage, and guide its expression.*

Soil and seed, seed and soil in balance and in harmony.

The Twenty-Four Dynamics
of Thriving Youth

My Child

- ☐ 1. My child knows his spark (or sparks).
- ☐ 2. My child is intrinsically motivated to pursue his spark.
- ☐ 3. My child uses discretionary time to explore his spark.
- ☐ 4. My child shows signs of passion for his spark.
- ☐ 5. My child takes initiative to exercise his spark.
- ☐ 6. My child likes to be stretched and challenged.
- ☐ 7. My child looks for opportunities to use his spark.
- ☐ 8. My child has a lot of positive energy when exploring his spark.

The People and Places in My Child's Life

- ☐ 9. My child's parents or caregivers know and affirm her spark.
- ☐ 10. My child has three or more adults who know and affirm her spark.
- ☐ 11. My child has several caring adults in her life who help her spark grow.
- ☐ 12. My child has several adults who provide or find opportunities to express her spark.
- ☐ 13. My child has several adults who push her to keep moving forward.
- ☐ 14. There are several adults in my child's life who model a life of spark.
- ☐ 15. My child's school and community offer opportunities to explore and develop sparks.
- ☐ 16. My child has friends who affirm and encourage her spark.

How My Child Changes People and Places

☐ 17. My child reaches out to adults to ask for support or guidance.

☐ 18. My child finds or creates opportunities to express the spark.

☐ 19. My child uses his spark to make life better for others.

☐ 20. My child helps other youth find and embrace their spark.

How People and Places Change My Child

☐ 21. Caring people and places strengthen my child's passion and energy.

☐ 22. Caring people and places strengthen my child's motivation.

☐ 23. Caring people and places help my child see the beauty of his spark.

☐ 24. Caring people and places help connect my child's spark to the needs of the world.

THE CHALLENGE TO AMERICA

We care a great deal about being good parents. But sometimes we get confused about what successful parenting looks like. How do we know if we are doing well? It is all too common in America to count trophies, test scores, popularity, or the status of colleges to which our kids are admitted as ways of knowing if we are doing well. None of these have much to do with a life of quality or contribution.

Keep the Spark Lit

Good parenting, I would suggest, has more to do with helping our young people find their spark, their essence. If trophies and high test scores result, that's icing on the cake. The point is, of course, that lives of joy and energy and hope and generosity are shaped from the inside out. We need to help our children find and express their light first. The rest will fall into place.

Our nation is not organized to help our young people find and express their light. Recall that only a small minority of America's youth have the spark champions they need to thrive. In fact, we are pretty clever in how we snuff out the light.

- When we create high-stakes-performance schools that care only about test scores, we snuff out the light.

- When we abandon kids in low-income communities, we snuff out the light.

- When adults become suspicious and fearful of teenagers, we deprive our young of the spark champions they so desperately need.

- When we segregate adults and youth into different living and learning spaces, we deprive our young of the sustained connections they need to flourish.

- When school districts are forced to trim back on arts, music, and drama, we undermine the most common source of sparks in our nation.

Share a Vision for Spark

At the root of our national dilemma is a lack of vision. We simply do not have a frame of reference, a shared understanding, a common dream, for growing great kids. Without a shared vision rooted in promoting the potential of each and every child, we create, at best, national and community initiatives designed to put out fires.

We fear drug and alcohol use by our young, so we invest heavily in prevention programs. We fear violence in communities and schools, so we write up rules and install weapon detectors that are meant to curb it. We fear losing our top-dog role in the global economy, so we create big initiatives to drill science and math skills into our young.

These efforts hardly represent a social or political interest in growing hopeful, focused, thriving kids. They may help some youth survive adolescence, but they do not in any way help youth develop as participants in our society.

The vision our nation needs begins with seeing each child as precious and filled with potential. The vision recognizes that all citizens have the responsibility and capacity to nurture this potential. The vision calls for schools and communities to know each of their young people so well that they can nurture and benefit from each child's spark. The vision recognizes that governmental policy requires deep transformation, moving from a preoccupation with preventing problems to a proactive investment in promoting human potential.

How will this vision emerge, and who will be its shapers and promulgators? I think America's parents must be the critical actors. As more and more of us come to know and value the sparks within our children, we will find a shared voice, a shared vocabulary, a shared concern for how well our neighborhoods and schools and communities embrace the light within each of our young people.

My fondest hope is that you will become a spark champion both for your child and for all our children. As we find and support each other, we can get to that tipping point where our nation commits to ensuring that all our young people are on the path to a hopeful future.

Spark
Resources

Teenage Sparks
A Rich National Tapestry

Our interviews with several thousand American teenagers have yielded a rich tapestry of sparks—more than two hundred.

We are interested in expanding the list of sparks. If you know of another one, post it on our Web site at www.ignitesparks.com.

1. Music: Instrumental

1.1   Piano

· 1.2   Guitar

1.3   Violin

1.4   Cello

1.5   Saxophone

1.6   Clarinet

1.7   Bass

1.8   Drums

1.9   Percussion

1.10   Trumpet

1.11   Trombone

1.12   Harmonica

1.13   Accordion

1.14   Other

2. Music: Conducting/Directing

2.1   Directing a choir

2.2   Directing a band

2.3   Conducting an orchestra

2.4   Other

3. Music: Composition

3.1   Writing song lyrics

3.2   Composing musical scores

3.3   Creating beats, composing hip-hop or rap

3.4   Other

4. Music: Performance

4.1   Singing in a choir

4.2   Singing, playing solo

4.3   Band

4.4   Orchestra

4.5   Other

5. Art

5.1   Painting

5.2   Drawing

5.3   Sketching

5.4   Sculpture

5.5   Graphic art

5.6   Pottery

5.7   Illustrating

5.8   Other

6. Writing

6.1   Poetry

6.2   Plays

6.3   Stories

6.4   Fiction

6.5   Nonfiction

6.6   Journaling

6.7   Other

7. Dance/Movement

7.1   Modern dance

7.2   Ballroom dancing

7.3   Cheerleading

7.4   Martial arts

7.5   Break dancing

7.6   Other

8. Other Creative Arts

8.1   Cooking

8.2   Sewing

8.3   Fashion design

8.4   Knitting

8.5   Other

9. Building and Design

9.1   Woodworking

9.2   Carpentry

9.3   Cabinetry

9.4   Construction

9.5   Drafting

9.6   Architecture

9.7   Other

10. Leadership

10.1   Problem solving

10.2   Bringing people together

10.3   Motivating people

10.4   Conflict resolution

10.5   Student government

10.6   Engagement in civic decision making

10.7   Membership on committees and boards

10.8   Other

11. Entrepreneurship

11.1   Creating business plans

11.2   Marketing

11.3   Sales

11.4   Management

11.5   Creating inventions

11.6   Developing new products

11.7   Designing services

11.8   Other

12. Sports and Athletics

12.1   Basketball

12.2   Football

12.3   Soccer

12.4   Tennis

12.5   Golf

12.6   Baseball

12.7   Softball

12.8   Running

12.9   Skateboarding

12.10   Skiing

12.11   Rowing

12.12   Horseback riding

12.13   Wrestling

12.14   Gymnastics

12.15   Bowling

12.16   Hockey

12.17   Archery

12.18   Conditioning

12.19   Swimming

12.20   Volleyball

12.21   Weight lifting

12.22   Other

13. Learning

13.1   Science

13.2   Math

13.3   Archaeology

13.4   History

13.5   Literature

13.6   Languages

13.7   Political science

13.8   Religion

13.9   Psychology

13.10   Anthropology

13.11   Geography

13.12   Sociology

13.13   Other

14. Teaching and Instructing

14.1   Swimming

14.2   Rock climbing

14.3   First aid

14.4   CPR

14.5   Computers

14.6   Team sports

14.7   Individual sports

14.8   Academic subjects (such as math, history, or science)

14.9   Languages

14.10   Other

15. Relationships

15.1   Making friends

15.2   Supporting friends

15.3   Being a peacemaker

15.4   Empathy

15.5   Studying people

15.6   Other

16. Serving, Helping, Volunteering

16.1   Making my community better

16.2   Volunteering

16.3   Helping people

16.4   Helping children

16.5   Tutoring

16.6   Mentoring

16.7   Counseling

16.8   Other

17. Nature, Ecology, Environment

17.1   Exploring the natural world

17.2   Protecting endangered species

17.3   Protecting wildlife

17.4   Conservation

17.5   Floral arranging

17.6   Growing flowers

17.7   Preservation

17.8   Landscaping

17.9   Gardening

17.10 Other

18. Animals

18.1   Raising animals

18.2   Caring for animals

18.3   Training animals

18.4 Animal medicine

18.5 Other

19. Computers

19.1 Keyboarding

19.2 Programming

19.3 Software development

19.4 Hardware

19.5 Computer repair

19.6 Computer graphics

19.7 Web page design

19.8 Other

20. Comedy

20.1 Making people laugh

20.2 Telling jokes

20.3 Writing sketches

20.4 Improvisation

20.5 Other

21. Speech

21.1 Public speaking

21.2 Debate

21.3 Broadcasting

21.4 Other

22. Spirituality

22.1 Meditation

22.2 Worship

22.3 Ritual

22.4   Sacred music

22.5   Studying sacred texts

22.6   Experiences of unity and harmony

22.7   Experiences of transcendence

22.8   Practice (yoga, for example)

22.9   Prayer

22.10 Other

23. Drama, Theater

23.1   Acting

23.2   Directing

23.3   Lighting

23.4   Set design

23.5   Other

24. Photography and Film

24.1   Nature photography

24.2   Filmmaking

24.3   Videography

24.4   Animation

24.5   Portrait photography

24.6   Movie production

24.7   Other

25. Being Committed to Living in a Specific Way

25.1   Joy

25.2   Passion

25.3   Tolerance

25.4   Caring

25.5 Optimism

25.6 Idealism

25.7 Other

26. Reading

26.1 Fiction

26.2 Poetry

26.3 Nonfiction

26.4 Memoirs

26.5 Biography

26.6 Autobiography

26.7 Other

27. Advocacy

27.1 Environment

27.2 Children

27.3 Social justice

27.4 School reform

27.5 Other

28. Family

28.1 Family history

28.2 Helping family

28.3 Celebrating family

28.4 Being with family

28.5 Other

29. Outdoor Life

29.1 Fishing

29.2 Hunting

29.3 Camping

29.4 Hiking

29.5 Bicycling

29.6 Other

30. Journalism

30.1 Newscasting

30.2 Newswriting

30.3 News editing

30.4 Radio and TV production

30.5 Other

31. Mechanics, Engineering

31.1 Electronics

31.2 Auto mechanics

31.3 Car audio

31.4 Bridge, highway design

31.5 Machine repair

31.6 Customizing

31.7 Other

32. Solving Social Problems

32.1 Global warming

32.2 Poverty

32.3 Racism

32.4 At-risk children

32.5 Pollution

32.6 Homelessness

32.7 Other

What Kids Need to Succeed

The 40 Developmental Assets (Ages 12 to 18 Years)

Search Institute has identified the following building blocks that help young people grow up healthy, caring, and responsible. More than three million sixth- to twelfth-grade youth have been surveyed in the United States and Canada since 1989, and every year, more young people continue to have their asset levels measured.

Search Institute research reveals that the more Developmental Assets young people have, the less likely they are to get into trouble (which we call risky behaviors), the more likely they are to act in positive ways (thriving indicators), and the more likely they will bounce back from difficulties (resiliency).

EXTERNAL ASSETS

Support

1. **Family support**—Family life provides high levels of love and support.

2. **Positive family communication**—Young person and her or his parent(s) communicate positively, and young person is willing to seek parent's advice and counsel.

3. **Other adult relationships**—Young person receives support from three or more nonparent adults.

4. **Caring neighborhood**—Young person experiences caring neighbors.

5. **Caring school climate**—School provides a caring, encouraging environment.

6. **Parent involvement in schooling**—Parent(s) are actively involved in helping young person succeed in school.

Empowerment

7. **Community values youth**—Young person perceives that adults in the community value youth.

8. **Youth as resources**—Young people are given useful roles in the community.

9. **Service to others**—Young person serves in the community one hour or more per week.

10. **Safety**—Young person feels safe at home, at school, and in the neighborhood.

Boundaries & Expectations

11. **Family boundaries**—Family has clear rules and consequences, and monitors the young person's whereabouts.

12. **School boundaries**—School provides clear rules and consequences.

13. **Neighborhood boundaries**—Neighbors take responsibility for monitoring young people's behavior.

14. **Adult role models**—Parent(s) and other adults model positive, responsible behavior.

15. **Positive peer influence**—Young person's best friends model responsible behavior.

16. **High expectations**—Both parent(s) and teachers encourage the young person to do well.

Constructive Use of Time

17. **Creative activities**—Young person spends three or more hours per week in lessons or practice in music, theater, or other arts.

18. **Youth programs**—Young person spends three or more hours per week in sports, clubs, or organizations at school and/or in community organizations.

19. **Religious community**—Young person spends one or more hours per week in activities in a religious institution.

20. **Time at home**—Young person is out with friends "with nothing special to do" two or fewer nights per week.

INTERNAL ASSETS

Commitment to Learning

21. **Achievement motivation**—Young person is motivated to do well in school.

22. **School engagement**—Young person is actively engaged in learning.

23. **Homework**—Young person reports doing at least one hour of homework every school day.

24. **Bonding to school**—Young person cares about her or his school.

25. **Reading for pleasure**—Young person reads for pleasure three or more hours per week.

Positive Values

26. **Caring**—Young person places high value on helping other people.

27. **Equality and social justice**—Young person places high value on promoting equality and reducing hunger and poverty.

28. **Integrity**—Young person acts on convictions and stands up for her or his beliefs.

29. **Honesty**—Young person "tells the truth even when it is not easy."

30. **Responsibility**—Young person accepts and takes personal responsibility.

31. **Restraint**—Young person believes it is important not to be sexually active or to use alcohol or other drugs.

Social Competencies

32. **Planning and decision making**—Young person knows how to plan ahead and make choices.

33. **Interpersonal competence**—Young person has empathy, sensitivity, and friendship skills.

34. **Cultural competence**—Young person has knowledge of and comfort with people of different cultural/racial/ethnic backgrounds.

35. **Resistance skills**—Young person can resist negative peer pressure and dangerous situations.

36. **Peaceful conflict resolution**—Young person seeks to resolve conflict nonviolently.

Positive Identity

37. **Personal power**—Young person feels he or she has control over "things that happen to me."

38. **Self-esteem**—Young person reports having a high self-esteem.

39. **Sense of purpose**—Young person reports that "my life has a purpose."

40. **Positive view of personal future**—Young person is optimistic
   about her or his personal future.

Note: This list may be reproduced for educational, noncommer-
cial purposes only. Copyright © 2008 by Search Institute, 615 First
Avenue NE, Suite 125, Minneapolis, MN 55413; 800/888-7828;
www.search-institute.org. Developmental Assets is a registered
trademark of Search Institute. Visit Search's Web site to download
the free list of 40 Developmental Assets in other languages and for
other age groups.

Key Spark Resources

RECOMMENDED NONFICTION BOOKS

The following books are helpful in learning more about each of the five steps. These are only a few of the many recommended books; visit www.ignitesparks.com to download free recommended resources lists for many different aspects of spark and for different age groups.

Step One: Recognize the Power of Sparks

Finding Your Own North Star, by Martha Beck (New York: Three Rivers Press, 2001). The Harvard-trained sociologist and career counselor invites you to explore your heart's desires and, in her hallmark entertaining style, helps you evaluate your current pleasures and pains, teaches the process of listening to the body's directional cues, and provides an intriguing "Map of Change" to reach the payoff: a love affair with life.

Finding Flow: The Psychology of Engagement with Everyday Life, by Mihaly Csikszentmihalyi (New York: Basic Books, 1997). One of the more challenging of the recommended selections, this book is invaluable because in addition to being supported by scientifically valid, large-scale studies, it asks the essential question, "What is the good life?" This esteemed psychologist expounds on how to find flow (another word for spark) in different domains of everyday life.

Step Two: Know Your Own Teenager

Magic Trees of the Mind: How to Nurture Your Child's Intelligence, Creativity, and Healthy Emotions from Birth Through Adolescence, by Marian Diamond, PhD, and Janet Hopson (New York: Penguin, 1999). This book reveals how your child's brain physically responds to environmental influences and how to bring out the best in your teenager.

Nurture by Nature: Understand Your Child's Personality Type—and Become a Better Parent, by Paul D. Tieger and Barbara Barron-Tieger (New York: Little, Brown, 1997). Find practical advice on how to determine your child's personality (and your own) and how to parent so that you both thrive.

Step Three: Help Discover and Reveal Your Teen's Sparks

Finding Your True Calling: The Handbook for People Who Still Don't Know What They Want to Be When They Grow Up—But Can't Wait to Find Out, edited by Valerie Young (Changing Course, 2002). With a number of real-life examples and contributions from experts and motivators in the field, Young guides you in the process of identifying dreams and thinking outside the box to find meaningful ways to make a living that fit with your talents and deepest desires.

The Path to Purpose: Helping Our Children Find Their Calling in Life, by William Damon (New York: Free Press, 2008). The culmination of thirty years of work as a research psychologist, this book addresses what the author calls the most pervasive problem of the day: a sense of emptiness that keeps many young people adrift at a time in their lives when they should be defining aspirations and making progress toward fulfillment.

What Color Is Your Parachute? For Teens: Discovering Yourself, Defining Your Future, by Richard Nelson Bolles and Carol Christen (Berkeley, Calif.: Ten Speed Press, 2006). Discover practical ways to blend your teenager's strengths with what he or she can use them for in the future.

Step Four: Be the Captain of Your Teen's Spark Team

All Kids Are Our Kids, by Peter L. Benson (San Francisco: Jossey-Bass, 2006). The author of *Sparks* explains how to be involved in your teenager's life in effective ways, how to get others involved in your child's life, and how to make a difference in the lives of other teenagers.

Big Questions, Worthy Dreams: Mentoring Young Adults in Their Search for Meaning, Purpose, and Faith, by Sharon Daloz Parks (San Francisco: Jossey-Bass, 2000). A guidebook written by a theology professor who welcomes the role of mentors for twenty-somethings; her emphasis is on spirituality rather than traditional religion and on helping young people in their twenties find a focus as well as a place within themselves and society.

Exuberance: The Passion for Life, by Kay Redfield Jamison (New York: Random House, 2004). Defining the contagious nature of exuberance as a state characterized by high mood and high energy, the author offers diverse examples of real people, such as conservationist John Muir, physicist Richard Feynman, and U.S. presidents Theodore Roosevelt and FDR, as well as beloved fictional ones like Mary Poppins and Peter Pan, making the case that "the exuberant act."

Step Five: Keep Your Teen's Spark Lit

The Web of Life: Weaving the Values That Sustain Us, by Richard Louv (Berkeley, Calif.: Conari Press, 1996). With warmth and wisdom, the author sends a passionate call for rebuilding community and family life and recognizing the important roles of time, spirit, nature, community, family, and friendship in preserving the values that sustain us; here is a springboard for taking time and making space in order to discover our individual sparks.

The Intuitive Spark: Bringing Intuition Home to Your Child, Your Family, and You, by Sonia Choquette (Carlsbad, Calif.: Hay House, 2007). The author zeroes in on the important role intuition plays in recognizing the inner spark and honoring what is authentic, so the content features a wealth of anecdotes and exercises that have worked for the highly intuitive author as both a parent and a counselor, helping young people, especially, discover and sustain confidence, creative expression, and inner peace.

Passionaries, by Barbara R. Metzler (Philadelphia: Templeton Foundation Press, 2006). This helpful book highlights teenagers and adults who follow their passion (or spark) and make a difference in the world.

INSPIRING SPARK BOOKS FOR TWELVE- TO FOURTEEN-YEAR-OLDS

Fire in the Heart: A Spiritual Guide for Teens, by Deepak Chopra (New York: Simon Pulse, 2004). A boy meets a mysterious old man, Baba, who, for four days, ignites sparks of spiritual insight and offers guidance about how to live in and change the world. A complement to this engaging overview that answers teens' specific questions is *Teens Ask Deepak: All the Right Questions* (New York: Simon & Schuster, 2005), by the same author.

The Loud Silence of Francine Green, by Karen Cushman (New York: Clarion Books, 2006). Eighth-grader Francine begins to question her values and silence, to struggle with whether to honor the spark within and act on her convictions, as she witnesses the expulsion of a transfer student who dares to question authority in this novel set at the beginning of the Cold War, a period of blacklisting and pervasive fear that strikes a chord in a post-9/11 world.

Hoot, by Carl Hiaasen (New York: Macmillan, 2004). You will find yourself engaged in an ecological mystery, featuring miniature owls, the All-American Pancake House to be built over their burrows, and unlikely allies: three middle school kids determined to beat the screwed-up adult system and the so-called development.

Heat, by Mike Lupica (New York: Puffin, 2007). This warmhearted story of Michael Arroyo, the star pitcher of his Little League team, revolves around his dream to one day play in Yankee Stadium like fellow Cuban refugee, major leaguer El Grande, but his father's death and a bitter rival's rumor that benches Michael during the Little League World Series threatens to extinguish Michael's spark.

The Giver, by Lois Lowry (Boston: Houghton Mifflin, 1993). In this Newbery Medal–winning fantasy and popular coming-of-age story, the young protagonist, raised in a seemingly perfect future society, has the courage to question and to quest as he wrestles with issues of freedom and free will; this book provides a great springboard for discussion.

Dairy Queen, by Catherine Murdock (New York: Graphia, 2007). For fifteen-year-old farm girl and jock D.J., football is her passion, and the summer that she takes on training the quarterback of a rival school's football team is one of important self-discovery.

My Life in Dog Years, by Gary Paulsen (New York: Yearling, 1999). Paulsen's autobiographical account of his love for dogs shows how they keep his spark alive. The book celebrates eight memorable pets, including the adopted Great Dane who stars in a wildly funny chapter—a book sure to charm fellow animal lovers and the author's many fans alike.

A Single Shard, by Linda Sue Park (New York: Clarion, 2001). A riveting read set in twelfth-century Korea, this Newbery Medal winner recounts the fate of an orphan raised by a homeless man and introduced to the craft of pottery by a demanding master whose own work and character ultimately inspire his apprentice to greatness.

All of the Above, by Shelley Pearsall (New York: Little, Brown Young Readers, 2008). A seventh-grade math teacher in a "dead-end" middle school challenges several initially uninspired and reluctant students to build a tetrahedron to break the Guinness world record (as in a similar real-life event in 2002); the impact on students and community is inspirational.

Generation Fix: Young Ideas for a Better World, by Elizabeth Rusch (Hillsboro, Ore.: Beyond Words, 2002). These real-life stories feature teens who are feeding the hungry, caring for the sick, protecting the environment, and fighting for equality, as they use amazing solutions they've created and inspire readers to recognize and honor their own sparks to make a difference.

Rain Is Not My Indian Name, by Cynthia Leitich Smith (New York: HarperCollins, 2001). Unwilling (and emotionally unable) to register for and participate in a summer Native American youth camp in the aftermath of a best friend's death, Rain, the main character, finally reenters the world through the lens of her camera, documenting the camp experience for the community newspaper.

Surviving the Applewhites, by Stephanie S. Tolan (New York: HarperCollins, 2002). Jake, a thirteen-year-old delinquent, suddenly finds himself living with an eccentric (and laugh-out-loud funny) family, each having an artistic bent (with the exception of one daughter who hates their loosey-goosey ways); in the midst of the organized madness, Jake discovers his own hidden spark and unique potential, as does his peer, E.D.

American Born Chinese, by Gene Luen Yang (New York: First Second, 2007). Three plotlines in this graphic novel cleverly converge in a powerful climax to an often humorous and affecting commentary about race, identity, and self-acceptance; the main character, Jin Wang, is initially willing to do anything to fit in with his white classmates in his American middle school, but ultimately realizes that there is no better feeling than honoring your own spark and being comfortable in your own skin.

INSPIRING SPARK BOOKS FOR FIFTEEN- TO TWENTY-YEAR-OLDS

The Absolutely True Diary of a Part-Time Indian, by Sherman Alexie (New York: Little, Brown Young Readers, 2007). This National

Book Award winner is a semiautobiographical chronicle of Arnold Spirit, a fourteen-year-old who was born with water on the brain and is the target of bullies, who loves to draw and play basketball—a spot-on, often humorous account, complete with teenage explicit language and true-to-life depictions of life on and off the rez, inspiring readers to explore identity and lift themselves out of the rough situations that they, like Arnold, may find themselves in. (Parental discretion advised.)

Hope Was Here, by Joan Bauer (New York: Puffin, 2005). In this Newbery Honor book, sixteen-year-old Hope is a waitress at the Welcome Stairways diner where her aunt (and guardian) is the talented cook, and it's in the little Wisconsin town they now call home that Hope feels inspired to help G. T. Stoop, battling leukemia, to run for election as mayor, as well as to develop a new sense of self and reinforce her "mission" as a waitress.

Shark Girl, by Kelly Bingham (Cambridge, Mass.: Candlewick, 2007). A gifted artist survives a shark attack at age fifteen, but loses a limb and must take an inner journey, as she physically heals, to regain a sense of self and to find a way to honor her talent.

In These Girls, Hope Is a Muscle, by Madeleine Blais (Boston: Atlantic Monthly Press, 1995). The true story of the Amherst Regional High School girls' basketball team has been dubbed "powerful," "funny, exciting, and moving," and "a must for anyone who has played a high school sport." Also about the quest for success and for respect, it's inspiring reading for teens, both male and female.

The Plain Janes, by Cecil Castellucci (San Diego: Minx, 2007). A quirky and comic graphic novel, underscoring the importance of self-expression and art, stars four friends (all named Jane) who form a secret club to liven up their town with what the local police dub "art attacks," in a story about outsiders that will appeal especially to comics readers and fans of soul-searching, realistic young adult fiction.

Crackback, by John Coy (New York: Scholastic, 2007). A talented football player who loves the game, Miles wrestles with his peers' steroid use, a coach who does not inspire his respect, family secrets, and a sense that there is more to life than the game.

The Kings Are Already Here, by Garret Freymann-Weyr (New York: Puffin, 2004). Phebe and Nikolai engage in their obsessions of ballet and chess, respectively, as they become friends while in Europe, and each must decide whether the price of being the best in their single-minded pursuits is worth the price, with one of them cementing the devotion to calling and the other changing direction.

The Impossible Will Take a Little While: A Citizen's Guide to Hope in a Time of Fear, by Paul Rogat Loeb (New York: Basic Books, 2004). Over sixty contributions (or spark-lers!) from great thinkers and doers in the world (including Bill McKibben, Vaclav Havel, Arundhati Roy, Marian Wright Edelman, Rumi, and Desmond Tutu) provide an antidote for teens who take a the-world-is-going-to-hell or what's-the-use-in-trying stance, as each, in his or her own way, can, from personal experience, unequivocally assert that every little bit counts, that ordinary people can make a difference, and that history is full of surprising victories of the weak over the strong.

Monster, by Walter Dean Myers (New York: Amistad, 1999). Sixteen-year-old Steve Harmon finds himself in prison and awaiting trial for murder as the lookout during a botched holdup; readers must weigh the evidence and issues related to the fate of the young aspiring filmmaker who records his trial as a screenplay and, in handwritten form, makes anguished entries in his journal about peer pressure, the choices one makes, the integrity of people, and different degrees of guilt. (Includes several references to violence and sexual assault.)

Cuba 15, by Nancy Osa (New York: Delacorte Books for Young Readers, 2005). It is her interest in and affinity for writing, for theater, and for her speech team's entry into an Original Comedy competition that sustain Violet Paz as her Cuban father insists that she take part in her own traditional Latina quinceañero (coming-of-age celebration for Hispanic females), complete with ruffled dress and tiara, and that ultimately inspire ideas in her for how to create a magical mix of cultures with old and new traditions at the celebration.

Doing Time: Notes from the Undergrad, by Rob Thomas (New York: Simon & Schuster, 1997). In this realistic work of fiction, each of ten short stories focuses on one high school student's mandatory two hundred hours of community service and the differing results and rewards accruing from each one's efforts.

True Believer, by Virginia Euwer Wolff (New York: Atheneum Books for Young Readers, 2001). Amid a range of distractions including an unattainable love interest and her mother's attraction to a new man, LaVaughn maintains her focus on finding a way out of her present neighborhood through a future college education; this National Book Award winner is the second in a trilogy that reviewers have called "transcendent," "truthful," "touching and sympathetic," "groundbreaking," and "uplifting."

WEB SITES FOR TEENAGERS PURSUING THEIR SPARK

An audio journal of your spark. Document your days as other teens are who are documenting their lives for public radio by keeping an audio journal of more than thirty hours of raw tape. Then collaborate with an editor at National Public Radio for the program *All Things Considered*. Podcasts and photos of other teens' diaries are available at this site. Visit: www.radiodiaries.org/teenagediaries.html.

Your own online diary. Create your own online diary and e-mail address for the site, adding entries whenever you wish. It's free. Visit: www.diaryland.com.

Network with other spark-pursuing teenagers. Connect with other like-minded teens about such causes as animal rights, violence prevention, war and peace, arts and media, and poverty, and see how individuals and groups are already speaking up and acting in the world. Visit: www.youthnoise.com.

Volunteer Match. Get involved. This is the largest online network of participating nonprofits; it attracts thousands of volunteers of all ages every day who can match their available times, location, and specific interests and talents to specific volunteer opportunities and ways to serve others. Visit: www.volunteermatch.com.

Post your own blog. Create and post your own blog on this site for all ages. Visit: www.blogger.com/start.

Magnetic Poetry. Play with words without all the fuss of using tiny little magnets. Kits with related groups of words range from "Genius," "Shakespeare," and "Artist" to "High School," "My Friend," "Dog Lover," and "College." Visit: www.magneticpoetry.com/magnets.

Sparks for girls. This bilingual (Spanish and English) site covers everything from "Starting a Business" and "Saving the World" to "Table Manners" and "Mentors," with access to current news about girls, advice about issues like bullying, a monthly newsletter, and resources. Visit: www.educatingjane.com/Girls/girls.htm.

Youth advocacy. The National Youth Rights Association defends the civil and human rights of young people in the United States and empowers teens to work on their own behalf. Find information on such issues as lowering the voting age, repealing government curfews, and fighting age discrimination. Visit: www.youthrights.org.

Youth activism. At this site, youth activism rules with news stories like "Top 10 Youth Activism Victories in 2007" and "The Youth Guide to Politics"; you can sign up to receive the most popular stories once a week or submit a story to be published and paid for on WireTap. Visit: www.wiretapmag.org/index.html.

Sheltered Reality. This organization highlights teen drumming troupes across the country learning about leadership, passion, and success through performing. Read the About Us page. Visit: www.sheltered-reality.org.

WEB SITES FOR ADULTS MODELING THEIR SPARK

The Spirited Woman. Nancy Mills does workshops across the country and runs this Web site to encourage women to discover and pursue their passions. Visit: www.thespiritedwoman.com.

Life Shine Coaching. This is Michelle and Bill Stimpson's help-ful site. Check out the good content about finding your spark, espe-cially in the Newsletters and Success Stories sections. Visit: www. lifeshinecoaching.com.

Peggy McColl. McColl is an expert on goal setting and the author of *The Destiny Switch*, which was recently a *New York Times* best-seller. There are articles on the site about pursuing your dreams. Visit: www.destinies.com.

Doing Good Together. As family, volunteer together through the creative ideas listed on this Web site. Visit: www.doinggood together.org.

Ladies Who Launch. This national organization supports women as they start their own businesses. Visit: www.ladieswholaunch.com.

Loretta LaRoche. This motivational speaker has books and humorous presentations on eliminating stress and taking charge of your life. Visit: www.lorettalaroche.com.

You Can Do It. This book and companion Web site were created by the friends of a woman who died in 9/11. (It was her idea.) It's about encouraging women to live their biggest dreams. Visit: www. youcandoitbook.com.

Daymaker Movement. David Wagner owns Juut salons but also created the Daymaker Movement, showing people the many ways to make someone else's day using your own gifts. Visit: www. daymakermovement.com.

Cranium. Everyone has gifts and talents. Click on Everybody Shines when you visit: www.cranium.com. Also check out cofounder and "Grand Poo Bah" Richard Tait's list of books and movies that inspire him. Visit: www.cranium.com/rd/en/keeping_inspiration _alive.aspx.

Repotting. This Web site shows how to replant and repot your spark so that you can grow your passions later in life. Visit: www. repotting.com.

Monster. Uncover your strengths by taking this test. Visit: my.monster.com/JobStrengthProfile/Intro.aspx.

INSPIRING FILMS AND VIDEOS

Akeelah and the Bee (PG, 2006). A young girl from South Los Angeles discovers her spark for spelling and tries to make it to the National Spelling Bee, even though she constantly runs into major barriers and hurdles.

Andy Goldworthy's Rivers and Tides (Not rated, 2001). Follow sculptor Andy Goldworthy's journey as he creates works of art from nature.

Coach Carter (PG-13, 2005). Coach Ken Carter realizes that his basketball players need not only a spark for basketball but also a spark for succeeding in life (which many of them lack). Full of unusual twists and turns, this film shows that having a spark is one thing, but succeeding in life is another.

Finding Neverland (PG, 2004). This film tells the story of J. M. Barrie, the author of *Peter Pan*, and how his life inspired him to write and follow his spark.

Dead Poets Society (PG, 1989). Professor John Keating motivates his students to learn through his Dead Poets Society. As students open up their minds and begin to question the status quo, their lives change.

Freedom Writers (PG-13, 2007). Idealistic teacher Erin Gruwell finds herself trying to teach in a high school riddled with violence and gang activity. Over the course of the movie, Gruwell and her students discover an unusual spark.

Holes (PG, 2003). A boy is wrongly convicted and sent to a brutal desert detention camp where he joins other inmates in digging holes. In the process, they unravel a mystery and discover their sparks.

Mask (PG-13, 1985). Rocky Dennis, a seriously deformed yet warm and bright child, tries to figure out who he is in the world while his mother, Rusty, works to give him positive experiences that most people take for granted.

Millions (PG, 2004). When a bag of currency falls from the sky, five-year-old Damian learns what really drives people. Some people have a spark; others clearly don't.

Mr. Holland's Opus (PG, 1995). Musician and composer Glenn Holland becomes a high school music teacher to pay the rent. Over the years, he finds how music activities give young people more than just something useful to do with their time.

October Sky (PG, 1999). The true story of Homer Hickam, a coal miner's son who was inspired by the first Sputnik launch to take up rocketry against his father's wishes.

OT: Our Town (Not rated, 2002). Dominguez High School in California doesn't have any money, or even a stage. Yet two teachers and twenty-four students attempt to produce their own urban version of the play *Our Town*.

Secondhand Lions (PG, 2003). A shy boy discovers all kinds of fascinating sparks from his eccentric uncles in Texas, who have lived long, spark-filled lives.

Stand and Deliver (PG, 1987). Teacher Jaime Escalante uses unconventional teaching methods to transform young people who didn't think much of themselves or their future into some of the country's top algebra and calculus students. Based on a true story.

Together (PG, 2002). A violin prodigy and his father travel to Beijing, where the father pushes his son to succeed and the son questions his destiny.

Whale Rider (PG-13, 2002). A young Maori girl struggles to find her spark, a spark her grandfather refuses to recognize.

ORGANIZATIONS AND STUDIES

Spark champions. Visit the official Web site about sparks at www. ignitesparks.com.

Search Institute. This Minneapolis-based nonprofit organization created the concept of spark and developed research studies to reveal the impact of spark. For fifty years, Search Institute has been conducting research on what helps teenagers, children, families, and communities thrive. Visit: www.search-institute.org.

MVParents. All parents want to be "Most Valuable Parents" who help their children and teens make smart choices and avoid the pitfalls of growing up. Visit: www.mvparents.com.

The Center for Spiritual Development in Childhood and Adolescence. This global initiative seeks to advance the research and practice of this important and understudied domain of human development. Visit: www.SpiritualDevelopmentCenter.org.

Healthy Communities • Healthy Youth. There are now more than six hundred cities from around the world that are part of the Healthy Communities • Healthy Youth network. In each of these initiatives, teenagers rise up to help lead the change process. Each year, Search Institute sponsors the national Healthy Communities • Healthy Youth Conference. Hundreds of cities send teams of adults and youth to teach and learn about community transformation. It's the largest intergenerational, international conference held in the United States. Visit: www.search-institute.org/communities/hchy.html.

Building Strong Families: A Survey from YMCA of the USA and Search Institute on What Parents Need to Succeed. Parents of children and teenagers are "going it alone," without the support, encouragement, and networks that would make it easier to overcome the daily challenges of parenting, according to a poll of 1,005 parents by YMCA of the USA and Search Institute. Most parents interviewed generally feel successful as parents most of the time, and they do many things to help their children grow up strong and healthy. However, they say that more support and affirmation from others would really help them as parents. For a free copy of the study, visit: www.search-institute.org/families/bsf2002.html.

Building Strong Families for African Americans and Latino Parents. The vast majority of African American and Latino/Latina parents are working hard to raise strong, healthy, and successful children and adolescents, and most feel they are doing well as parents. Yet they are doing so in the face of multiple challenges in their communities and society. Furthermore, most have little support beyond their immediate family to help them as parents. Those are the major conclusions of this study of 685 African American parents and 639 Latino/Latina parents in the United States by Search Institute and YMCA of the USA. For a free copy of the study, visit: www.search-institute.org/families/bsf2004.html.

Grading Grown-Ups. American adults agree to a surprising degree on what kids need from them. Now, findings in two major national studies conducted by Search Institute show that only a small percentage of adults are deeply engaged in promoting the healthy development of young people outside their own families. These findings reveal agreement about some fundamental priorities for youth-adult relationships, as well as offer some eye-opening input on how and why adults are dropping the ball. Download a free copy of the study at www.search-institute.org/norms.

NOTES

Introduction

I use the concept of spark as a metaphor for that intrinsic capacity, skill, or competence that propels people toward exploration and expression. Spark is a necessary but not sufficient component of human thriving. Thriving necessitates the nurture and exploration of spark within several developmental contexts where adults see and prize it. Indeed, all human development is predicated on this dynamic interaction of self and context.

My theoretical and empirical work on adolescent thriving draws heavily on the positive youth development literature. This relatively new interdisciplinary approach to human development is premised on these ideas:

- All youth have the inherent capacity for growth.

- Positive growth is enabled when youth are embedded in nurturing relationships and environments.

- Youth are major actors in their own development.

There is now considerable scientific evidence that the promotion of positive development (by seeing young people as assets versus liabilities, reorganizing schools and youth organizations to focus on adult-youth relationship, and giving youth the space to explore their spark) is a powerful approach for boosting academic success and preventing risky behaviors. This line of theory and research is summarized in P. L. Benson, P. C. Scales, S. F. Hamilton, and A. Sesma Jr., "Positive Youth Development: Theory, Research and Applications," in W. Damon and R. M. Lerner (eds.), *Handbook of Child Psychology*, 6th ed., Vol. 1: *Theoretical Models of Human Development* (Hoboken, N.J.: Wiley, 2006).

My primary scientific colleague in developing theory and research on adolescent thriving is Peter C. Scales, PhD, senior social scientist at Search Institute. Together we have published a number of papers on this topic. A bibliography of these is available on the Search Institute Web site (www.search-institute.org).

Step One: Recognize the Power of Sparks

Here is a little more information about the three new studies of teenagers I premier in this book. First is the Gallup Poll. It was conducted by Search Institute for America's Promise—The Alliance for Youth to get a first-time benchmark for measuring to what degree our nation's young people receive the supports and opportunities they need to succeed. With Gallup, we polled, through a sophisticated telephone process, a nationally representative sample of two thousand twelve- to seventeen-year-olds and one parent of each of these teenagers. In these telephone interviews, we included questions on teenagers' sparks and the number of adults who know and support the spark. The poll included oversamples of Hispanic and African American families.

A second study Search Institute conducted was with Harris Interactive, a division of the Louis Harris polling firm. This was a twelve-question survey on thriving, with one question asking teenagers to describe their sparks in their own words. A national sample of more than a thousand eleven- to seventeen-year-olds participated. This study provided data on such issues as how often young people experience and express their sparks, and how much their specific developmental contexts—family, school, friends, congregations, youth organizations, neighborhoods—help them develop their sparks. Participants were also asked about school grades so that the connection between sparks and school success could be more deeply explored.

In a new area of science like this, it is useful (even critical) to gather qualitative data in which we listen and listen deeply to how people tell their own stories. With Just Kids, Inc., we designed a three-day Internet-based bulletin board discussion among teenagers. Of the 405 participants, all between fifteen and seventeen years of age, about 20 percent were African American or Hispanic. The moderated discussion gathered extensive qualitative information about how teens see their own sparks, how we can tell if a teenager is thriving, what obstacles teens face in expressing their sparks and what they do to overcome these, and how their environments help or hinder spark exploration. Here are some of the interview questions:

- Some teens your age have spark in their life. This spark can be a talent or interest like writing, an interest in science or nature, playing an instrument, being an artist or actor, leading others on a project, helping others, etc. This spark is something they are passionate about, really fires them up, gives them joy and energy, and is an important part of who they are. Teens with spark might have a goal they want to achieve with this spark and might have overcome obstacles and challenges in pursuing their spark. The spark is not just about things teens your age like to do, like hanging out with friends, dating, playing video games, or riding a bike. Spark is something that gives a person a sense that their life has purpose and makes them feel whole. Some teens might have more than one spark in their life. Do you feel you have a spark or several sparks?

- Please describe your spark (or sparks).

- Tell me how you feel when you are expressing your spark.

- Tell me about the things you do in order to help pursue your spark.

- Tell me about the obstacles you have had to overcome to pursue your spark.

- How can you tell when a teen has "spark"? What are they doing differently from other teens their age who don't have "spark"? How are they acting differently?

You have seen many quotes from these interviews throughout *Sparks*. My thanks go out, of course, to the thirty-five hundred young people who participated in these three studies. The hope and possibility in their lives are what this book seeks to describe. My fondest wish is that *Sparks* serves as an antidote to our bad habit of demonizing teenagers in the press and in public policy.

The William Damon book I reference is *Greater Expectations: Overcoming the Culture of Indulgence in Our Homes and Schools* (New York: Free Press, 1996).

Step Two: Know Your Own Teenager

This chapter covers a lot of territory on adolescent development. Here are some recommended readings on specific topics.

On the capacity of teenagers to thrive, see Richard Lerner, *The Good Teen* (New York: Random House, 2007).

We know a lot about how youth are becoming disconnected from adult relationships and social institutions. In his book *The Path to Purpose: Helping Our Children Find Their Calling in Life* (New York: Free Press, 2008), William Damon powerfully articulates the ways youth experience a profound sense of emptiness in their lives.

His concept of purpose and my concept of sparks are clearly tied to each other. If you like either concept, you have to read this book.

Spark, I would argue, is a capacity within all young people. It knows no economic bounds. However, the ways obstacles and opportunities emerge can vary quite a bit. We know a lot about the persistence of poverty in the United States and the way it can crush dreams. But we also see stories of success based usually on a powerful sense of spark, a willingness to move forward despite the odds, and the presence of one or more caring adults who model and support the expression of spark. Less visible are the issues faced by children of privilege. Here, the family and social demands to be successful can bury the spark. I recommend Madeline Levine's *The Price of Privilege: How Parental Influence and Material Advantage Are Creating a Generation of Disconnected and Unhappy Kids* (New York: HarperCollins, 2006).

To access Reed Larson's fine thinking on adolescent pathways, see his "Toward a Psychology of Positive Youth Development" in the January 2000 issue of *American Psychologist* (pp. 170–183).

For information about the exciting topic of brain development, I recommend an article by Ronald Dahl. He's a professor of psychiatry and pediatrics at the University of Pittsburgh Medical Center. It's titled "Adolescent Brain Development: A Period of Vulnerabilities and Opportunities," published in the *Annals of the New York Academy of Sciences*, 2004, pp. 1–22. David Walsh, PhD, has written a very useful interpretation of this literature for parents. It's called *Why Do They Act That Way? A Survival Guide to the Adolescent Brain for You and Your Teen* (New York: Free Press, 2004).

On the theory, research, and practice of the 40 Developmental Assets, see P. L. Benson, *All Kids Are Our Kids: What Communities Must Do to Raise Caring and Responsible Children and Adolescents* (San Francisco: Jossey-Bass, 2006). At www.search-institute.org, you will find dozens of very practical resources for building assets in your family and community.

Step Three: Help Discover and Reveal Your Teen's Sparks

Data for this chapter come from the Search Institute spark surveys mentioned in the notes for Step One. In addition, the list of sparks is a shortened version of the more extensive list that appears in the Spark Resource "Teenage Sparks: A Rich National Tapestry."

Some of the wonderful stories about how and where kids can find their spark are summarized, with permission, from *Passionaries: Turning Compassion into Action,* by B. R. Metzler (West Conshohocken, Penn.: Templeton Foundation Press, 2006).

You can find one of the many stories about Rick and Dick Hoyt on the CNN Web site at www.cnn.com/US/9911/29/hoyt.family.

Step Four: Be the Captain of Your Teen's Spark Team

The story of Sashe Dimitroff, used here with permission, comes from a wonderful set of narratives in B. Barrett, A. Annis, and D. Riffey (eds.), *Little Moments, Big Moments: Inspirational Stories of Big Brothers and Big Sisters and the Magic They Create* (Gilbert, Ariz.: Magical Moments, 2004).

I love books that portray young people as growing, contributing, and thriving. Here's another: J. Pelise (ed.), *Kid Stories: Biographies of 20 Young People You'd Like to Know* (Minneapolis: Free Spirit, 1991).

Lynn Stambaugh's story was originally published in *Assets* magazine, Autumn 1996, p. 5.

Step Five: Keep Your Teen's Spark Lit

Two thinkers from whom I learn a lot are quoted in this chapter. For more of Parker Palmer's thinking, I'd recommend *A Hidden Wholeness: The Journey Toward an Undivided Life* (2004) and *Let Your Life Speak* (1999), both published by Jossey-Bass.

Joseph Campbell's books on the myths of the world create an impressive body of work. A great way to get started is to read *The Power of Myth* (New York: Doubleday, 1988). It's a long interview of Campbell by Bill Moyers.

The percentages of adult relationships are drawn from unpub-
lished survey data from *Search Institute Profiles of Student Life: Atti-
tudes and Behaviors*. The sample includes148,189 students from U.S.
schools that administered the survey during 2003.

The story told by Rachel Naomi Remen is from the *Speaking of
Faith* online newsletter of December 12, 2007. *Speaking of Faith* is a
great weekly program on belief, meaning, ethics, and ideas from
American Public Media, broadcast on National Public Radio and
hosted by Krista Tippett.

The story of Mischa Zimmermann is told in more detail in *Rosie*
magazine, issue 5, 2001; Pilar Gonzales's story has appeared, among
other places, in *People* magazine, Dec. 24, 2007, p. 79.

ACKNOWLEDGMENTS

The creation of *Sparks* has been a seven-year journey, enabled at every phase by the generosity, encouragement, and support of an extraordinary family. To all of the King clan—Bob, Dottie, Cynthia, Alan, Pam, Brad, Jennifer, and Tim—I will be eternally grateful for your belief in me. To Cynthia King-Guffey, executive director of Thrive Foundation for Youth, I give thanks for inspiration, friendship, and the constant nudge to get the manuscript written. It all began in Santa Fe. Any King (by birth or marriage) has a lifetime seat on our bench.

To Jolene Roehlkepartain, I could not do this without you. You are a gem. Many thanks for your contributions.

This has been a team effort. My colleagues at Search Institute have been extraordinary. Peter Scales, as usual, has been my theory and research partner. The research premiered in *Sparks* owes much to his expertise and acumen. Kay Hong expertly watched over the writing and editing process and made invaluable contributions to the final manuscript. The incomparable Shelby Andress engaged young people in deep conversations about sparks, leading to compelling stories woven into the book. Nicole Hintz, Kathy Fraher, Claudia Hoffacker, and Brett Ellard contributed significantly to the work. And Gene Roehlkepartain helped guide and shape my thinking—as he always does. Thank you, team, from the bottom of my heart.

The impetus for *Sparks* came out of a multiyear, ongoing project on thriving youth that puts me in deep relationship with some extraordinary thinkers, scholars, and practitioners. I am indebted to Bill Damon, Duncan Campbell, Richard Lerner, Linda Wagener, Pamela King, Cynthia King-Guffey, and Jim Furrow for the years of moral, intellectual, and spiritual support. The Walton Family Foundation, the Campbell Foundation, the W.T. Grant Foundation, the Peninsula Foundation, the RGK Foundation, General Mills Foundation, AOL Time Warner Foundation, the Kansas Health Foundation, and the W.K. Kellogg Foundation helped enable our shared journey. And, of course, Thrive Foundation for youth has been the anchor, the inspiration, and the catalyst that has birthed this robust body of work on thriving. I am deeply grateful to Thrive and the broader network of support it has helped to generate.

Along the way, angels arrived at exactly the right time to nudge me forward. My thanks for timely wisdom from Arthur Schwartz, Willis Bright, Barbara Varenhorst, Tom Kieffer, Gregg Petersmeyer, Callie Guffey, Greg Kozmetsky, and Armin Brott, and for the support of the McKnight Foundation and my many friends within America's Promise—The Alliance for Youth.

My editor at Jossey-Bass, Alan Rinzler, truly strengthened the flow and prose. Thanks, Jim Levine, for building the bridge.

Undergirding *Sparks* are the stories of several thousand teenagers who participated in the research on thriving. This book stands on their shoulders, and I'm so grateful for their powerful testimony of what is possible.

My teachers and mentors—about living fully, about possibility, about courage and hope—are my family. Liv and Kai exude the concept of spark; I could not cherish them more. And Tunie Munson-Benson, my life partner, is always the one who sees most clearly and who most shows us how to live with passion and integrity. So Liv, Kai, and Tunie, my love and gratitude.

ABOUT THE AUTHOR

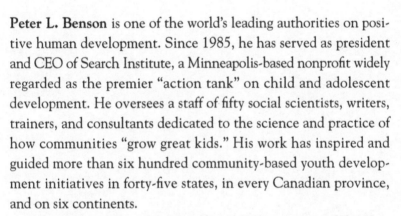

Peter L. Benson is one of the world's leading authorities on positive human development. Since 1985, he has served as president and CEO of Search Institute, a Minneapolis-based nonprofit widely regarded as the premier "action tank" on child and adolescent development. He oversees a staff of fifty social scientists, writers, trainers, and consultants dedicated to the science and practice of how communities "grow great kids." His work has inspired and guided more than six hundred community-based youth development initiatives in forty-five states, in every Canadian province, and on six continents.

Benson has advanced degrees from Yale University and the University of Denver and is the author or editor of more than a dozen books, including, most recently, *All Kids Are Our Kids: What Communities Must Do to Raise Caring and Responsible Children and Adolescents* and *The Handbook of Spiritual Development in Childhood and Adolescence*. Scholar, social visionary, and child advocate, he is a much-sought-after speaker, lecturer, and consultant. He has appeared on hundreds of television and radio broadcasts and frequently provides counsel to state and federal agencies.

He is the parent of two former teenagers and is married to Tunie Munson-Benson, an expert on children's literature. Their home in Minnetonka, Minnesota, once clean and tidy, is now overrun with grandchildren.

INDEX

t denotes table.